FEELING FREE

FEELING FREE

Archibald D. Hart

Fleming H. Revell Company
Old Tappan, New Jersey

Scripture quotations identified KJV are based on the King James Version of the Bible.

Scripture quotations identified NEB are from the New English Bible. © The Delegates of the Oxford University Press and the Syndics of the Cambridge University Press 1961 and 1970. Reprinted by permission.

Excerpt from THE VELVETEEN RABBIT by Margery Williams. Reprinted by permission of Doubleday & Company Inc.

Library of Congress Cataloging in Publication Data

Hart, Archibald D
    Feeling free.

    Includes bibliographical references and index.
    1. Emotions. 2. Psychology—Popular works.
3. Christian life—1960–   I. Title.
BF561.H38   152.4   78-26474
ISBN 0-8007-0973-X

Contents

Illustrations

Introduction

IF YOU ARE CONFUSED about your emotions and cannot make sense out of your feelings, this book is for you. If you are at all human, you are likely to be having trouble with your emotions in one of two ways—either you will be overwhelmed by them, or you will have found a way to overcontrol them.

If you are afraid of your emotions, it is probably because you neither understand them nor can you control them. You sense, rather, that *they* control you. Anger, hate, depression, guilt, jealousy, and the like have imprisoned you. There is nothing you seem to be able to do to free yourself from their grip once they have hold.

If you are a male, it is highly probable that, rather than being imprisoned by your emotions, you have imprisoned them. Notice, I do not say "tamed them," although you may feel it is pretty much the same thing. From your earliest years you have kept your emotions under tight control. You have been taught that it is weak to be emotional: "Crying is for sissies. Strong men can take everything that is dished out and never flinch." The result is, of course, that now you can't feel at all. You have built a cast-iron protective system that will withstand any emotional onslaught. You have imprisoned your emotions, but in the process have imprisoned yourself.

Which is better—to be overcontrolling of your feelings or to be controlled by them? In this book I seek to explore this issue carefully. I will try to show that neither of these extremes is desirable, and both are unhealthy. My message will be: You *can* control your emotions without imprisoning them, and they *can* be your friends and allies.

9

We easily misunderstand the role of emotions. For some, unpleasant emotions are devastating, while others are so afraid of their emotions that they become stunted and awkward and so inhibited by their inability to feel that they hardly know how to really live.

If you are a Christian believer, the problem is further aggravated because you can easily fall into the trap of believing that your emotions are not compatible with your life of faith. You can never allow yourself to be depressed, because you believe this is unchristian. You become totally immobilized by your anger, because you don't know what is the right and Christian thing to do.

You are not alone in this confusion. I am certain from my lectures to various church groups that there are many Christians who feel the same way. It is my purpose in this book to help you turn your emotions to your advantage.

To some extent this book may sound like just another self-help book, and I admit that it may appear that way on the surface. However, what I have to say can hardly be construed as self-help.

The most frustrating aspect of most self-help books (including books like *Your Erroneous Zones, Passages,* and *The Angry Book*) is that their central message is simply "It is entirely up to you." Up to a point this is true, but one important ingredient is missing as far as the Christian believer is concerned. It is the availability of powerful, life-changing therapeutic resources from without oneself. If we depended only and entirely on our inner resources, we would be hopelessly lost. We truly are in God's sight. The Scriptures are clear in telling us that the way of life in Christ is designed for our benefit, and we miss the central thrust of it all if we do not recognize and put into operation the life- and mind-changing resources that are provided. Our part is only one of cooperation—plainly and simply!

> Therefore, my brothers, I implore you by God's mercy to offer your very selves to him: a living sacrifice, dedicated and fit for his acceptance . . . . Adapt yourselves no longer to the pattern of this present world, but let your minds be remade and your whole nature thus transformed . . . .
>
> Romans 12:1, 2 NEB

Feelings are a part of life. We cannot escape them. We can, though, easily misunderstand them. In the first two chapters, therefore, I try to make sense out of our feelings. Need they be so painful? Do they have to be self-destructive? Can they not be turned to creative use and be made to work for us, thus enhancing our lives? I believe they can, and attempt to show what we must do to achieve this.

Chapter 3 is extremely important, and the ideas developed therein are continued as a thread throughout the remainder of the book. You can control your feelings if you learn how to control your stream of thought. What you believe, assume, expect, or perceive has important ramifications for how and what you feel. Therefore, the key to unlocking the mystery of your emotions lies in understanding these thought processes.

Chapters 4 through 9 deal with the specific emotional problems that I have encountered most frequently in my practice as a psychotherapist. The final chapter attempts to integrate it all by making a plea for reality in our personhood. We can only be *real* when we are authentic.

If you are a Christian, I have a special message for you. My bias throughout this book is obvious—and I make no apologies for it. Briefly stated it is that the Christian Gospel (Good News) contains the essential ingredients for emotional healthiness. Resources are provided which I believe can help you make your emotions work for you rather than against you. And it is because many Christians do not know how to do this that I have felt the need to write this book.

You can use this book in a number of ways—

• Its main use is as a personal study guide. Read it carefully and thoughtfully and put into practice my suggestions, and I know you will not be disappointed. I have used these techniques with scores of clients and groups and am confident that they work.

• You can use it as a study guide for small groups or with just a few friends in a home study group. Take time to discuss the contents and develop a system of accountability with each other to help you follow through on your endeavors.

• Adult Bible classes will find the book helpful as a source of discussion material, as each of the chapters can be coupled with portions of Scripture to give the contents a biblical emphasis. Additional reading material, including appropriate scriptural lessons, is suggested at the end of each chapter.

• Psychologists, counselors, and pastors may find the book to be helpful bibliotherapy for their clients. It can be used to guide clients through their emotions and provide a basis for the professional therapy.

In closing, let me sound two warnings:

1. If you can get no help from this book—or if in the reading of it you realize that your problem is a serious one—I encourage you to seek professional help without delay. Life is too short and too precious for you to waste it being imprisoned by your emotions. If you don't know where to go, consult your minister or doctor.

2. Don't rigidly follow the specific details of this book or become deadlocked over some minor detail you don't agree with. Pay attention mainly to the general principles and tailor the actions you must take to your specific situation.

I have been helped along my personal journey to emotional freedom by many colleagues and friends, too numerous to mention. To the Reverend Bernard Johanson, spiritual mentor over many years, I owe a debt of gratitude for spiritual insights. To Ron and Judi Capron, as well as to my wife, I owe a debt of gratitude for many personal insights. To Meg Lucas I owe what every writer owes to an efficient and tolerant secretary.

To my many clients, past and present, I owe a special debt of gratitude. You have trusted me with your minds and souls, and this has meant more to me than you can imagine. I have tried hard to conceal the identity of those I cite in the examples given in this book—and I am sure that there is no way you will be able to recognize yourselves, so don't try. I love you all too much to be guilty of callousness with what you have entrusted to me.

FEELING FREE

1

What Have You Done With Your Emotions?

AS I PEN THESE WORDS I have just come from spending a therapy session with a client. For more than half an hour she has cried pitifully, the first time she has done this in more than twenty years. I had struggled to get her to this point for more than six weeks. She had come many times to the brink of letting her tears flow, but fearfully she would retreat and hold them back. Now at last she has experienced a breakthrough and is experiencing some emotion again. She said to me, "You have no idea how good it is to feel like a real person again." A real person?

IIer forty-five years of life had been free of any serious hardship. Her parents were good people and had given her most of the material things she needed in life. But somehow she had never learned how to freely experience her emotions. From her earliest years she had thought that feelings should never be shown, and the best way not to show them was not to feel them. Her emotions had to be kept imprisoned. Skillfully she had taught herself how to hold down every hurt, every resentment, even her feelings of love, until she came to believe that she was incapable of ever experiencing any really deep feelings again. The unfortunate consequence of all of this was that she had become incapable of

15

forming any intimate relationships. Even her husband was kept at a safe emotional distance.

The therapeutic experience she had with me was both liberating and enlightening to her. She had found a way out of her emotional prison and discovered that she was not a real person unless she had the "freedom to feel."

Fortunately, not everyone has this serious a problem with feeling emotions. Some may experience a different problem—their feelings come too often and too powerfully. They may be so shaken up whenever their emotions overtake them that they have come to despise every feeling in their bodies, seeing only pain and potential destructiveness in their emotions.

The Two Extremes of Emotional Experience

We see, therefore, that there are two extremes of emotional experience and that both these extremes can produce an attitude toward emotion that is damaging. In both cases you believe that emotions are destructive, but in the first you learn how to avoid all feelings by convincing yourself that they don't exist at all and must therefore be denied or ignored. In the other extreme you just surrender to your emotions and put up no resistance whatever. In both extremes a most important point is missed, namely that emotions form an essential part of life and are the most important building blocks out of which happiness and enjoyment of life are built. To avoid feeling is to avoid life! To feel too much is to destroy life.

How do we strike a healthy balance? That is what this book is all about. In it I want to help you come to terms with your emotions. You may not be at either extreme, but I want you to come to the place where you will be "free to feel" and have a sense of still being in control of your feelings. Feelings are to be used to enhance your life, not destroy it. Unpleasant feelings can be avoided, if you so choose, without denying them; and your skill for doing this is not difficult to develop. If you are a Christian believer, I want you to come to realize that you have powerful resources at your disposal for developing a healthy mind and emotionally balanced life. You can have victory over yourself if you will utilize these resources.

The Problem of Emotion for the Christian

Many, if not most, Christians experience great conflict over their emotions. They find it very difficult to reconcile their experience of extreme feelings with their spirituality. This is, of course, all part of the larger problem of how to reconcile humanness with spiritualness, a problem that will be with us all our living days. But how does one bring together the emotional side of one's being with the spiritual side? Are they at war with each other? Do my emotions have to disturb my spiritual well-being? Are there some emotions I experience which are sinful because of the harm they cause me? These are some of the questions which plague the Christian clients I see, and they are all related to a much deeper question: "How can I be fully human, yet fully spiritual?"

I do not believe that God has called us to be superhumans, and one of the biggest mistakes we can make is to be misled into thinking that if we are Christian believers, we should never allow our emotions to get the better of us or that we should always be in complete control of every feeling. This idea leads to inauthenticity—a sort of phoniness which ruins our witness and destroys our effectiveness in helping others. It also sets us up for developing mental and emotional problems.

I once knew a woman missionary who was one of the most controlled and disciplined persons I had ever met. Nothing could ruffle her. She was always calm, never angry, and seemed to be able to handle all the big blows which life could deal her without getting upset. On the surface she gave the impression that she was a saint, but there was always something about her that made people afraid of her. Was she too perfect? Perhaps, but it was a perfection that hinted at inauthenticity.

While she was admired by most of those who knew her and with whom she worked, her witness tended to produce guilt more than anything else, as it made them feel so hopelessly inadequate in comparison with her. When others reflected on how they felt and then compared their reactions to hers, they felt hopeless failures. Rather than be attracted to her, they wanted to avoid her. Never would they share with her how they felt, nor could they ever go to her for counsel. What a sad situation!

Then one day she came to me for help. "Please don't tell anyone I have been to see you" was her opening remark, as she began to tell about how troubled she was by her emotions and how she had to work so hard at controlling and not displaying them for fear that she would be a "poor witness" to her Lord. I assessed her to be on the verge of a serious breakdown, and yet to the very last she was determined not to let anyone see it. Unfortunately, it was this determination that was to a large extent responsible for her problem. She was in emotional trouble precisely because she was preventing herself from giving free expression to her feelings. As I worked with her in psychotherapy, one of the things I did was to move her toward being much more authentic and honest about herself. She began to share her emotional struggles more openly with others and as a result found that she could better control them. The effect on her ministry was dramatic. She was now being perceived as more human, and her experiences became important to others, both from the modeling they provided for dealing with their emotions as well as the encouragement they gave.

We are not superhumans—and while it is not necessary for us to be dominated and disturbed by our emotions, it is also not necessary for us to be so afraid of them that we never ever allow them any expression. Emotions must be woven into our spiritual lives in such a way that they produce a harmonious and complementary pattern of wholeness. Our emotions are not fundamentally in conflict with our spirituality. Emotions themselves are not sinful. They do not have to disturb our spiritual well-being, but rather can be used to complement and enhance it.

Common Mistakes Christians Make in Their Emotions

In describing the experience of the woman missionary in the previous section, I tried to show that the mistake she was making was to cling to the belief that, in order to be the most effective witness, she had to deny and conceal her emotions. She feared that if others saw her emotional failures, she would be discredited. By doing this, she had robbed herself of all freedom to experience her feelings (known as "denial") and as a result had brought herself almost to the brink of a complete emotional breakdown.

It has been my experience that this is the most common mistake that Christians make regarding their emotions. They teach themselves very skillfully how to deny them. This is, of course, true also of people in general in our culture. From our earliest years we are taught that it is bad to be "emotional," and that feelings must, at all costs, never be shown. If it only stopped there, it would not be so bad, but we take it further, and in order for us not to show our feelings we train ourselves in not acknowledging them even to ourselves.

Let me illustrate this point by asking you to conduct a little experiment. The next time you are with someone, stop the conversation and ask him to describe to you how he is feeling at that instant. You will be surprised at how difficult it is for that person to describe accurately what he is feeling. I know, because as psychotherapists we try to get people to do this many times each day. Better still, stop yourself periodically and see whether you can describe to yourself how you are feeling. It will be just as difficult. Why? We have trained ourselves in the art of denial and the avoidance of feeling. We simply don't want to face our real inner selves where our feelings reside.

The problem can become further aggravated when you become a Christian. You move into a community of believers who, generally speaking, tend to resist the expression of real feelings. Partly this is because we are afraid of true intimacy; partly it's because this is how we perpetuate our own denial of feelings; and mainly it's because we fear being seen as a failure. "What will they think?" is the most neurosis-producing thought I know, and this idea—coupled with an unhealthy attitude toward any form of failure, especially within the Christian community—leads us to be very protective of our feelings and to avoid giving any acknowledgment to them. Take, for example, the problem of anger. At a meeting in which some controversial issue is being discussed, I have seen a deacon give lots of evidence that he is angry toward those round about him: flushed face, tight lips, and a loud voice. Yet when he is asked afterwards, "Were you angry?" he replies, "Never! I don't get angry that easily. I just wanted to tell them where they were going wrong!"

Later in this book I will discuss the reasons that it is necessary for you to have a healthy attitude towards failure, but let me merely say at this point that you are doing yourself a lot of harm if you cannot recognize and admit your feelings as they occur. This leads to emotional dishonesty and is self-destructive. The first step towards psychological health is emotional honesty, the ability to recognize and own up to your feelings. The second step is to allow yourself more freedom in the expression of your feelings, with the goal of becoming more "real" emotionally. Only then can you become the master of your emotions and not a slave to them. Only then can you stop imposing the most demanding and unrealistic expectations on your emotional state and find the freedom to be your true self.

Another common mistake many make, which is equally as destructive as denying and avoiding feelings, is to give in to their emotions in a defeatist way. "There is nothing I can do about feelings." "When I get that feeling all over me, I just go away and hide." "I'm useless to everybody." These are the comments I frequently hear from people who have given in. And obviously, since the people involved believe that there is nothing they can do about their feelings, their emotional state is perpetuated by this defeatist attitude until it weakens with time or something else happens to shake them out of it. One important reason why this defeatist attitude remains a problem is that the person involved does not see the important connection between his feelings and his thoughts. While feelings are *not* thoughts, feelings are on many occasions the *consequence* of our thoughts, and they can be perpetuated by what we think and say to ourselves. I will be stressing this point many times throughout this book and will devote a chapter to discussing it in fuller detail. Feelings are often the end product of a series of irrational self-statements, and we can avoid prolonging the feeling or even triggering it in the first place by carefully examining the content of our thoughts, challenging their validity, and changing their content. While our feelings have some physiological involvement in that our glands, heartbeat, breathing, and perspiration are all involved in our emotions, these physiological reactions are triggered in a complex way by our *thoughts*. This emphasis, which stresses the relationship between our thoughts (cognitions) and our emotions (affect), has recently received renewed interest in psychotherapy circles, and the methods of therapy which flow from it are proving to be very effective in dealing with emotional problems. I personally use these techniques extensively and find them to be consistent with much New Testament teaching, where a great emphasis is placed on the role of thoughts, attitudes, and faith in determining our well-being. Unpleasant emotions *can* be controlled to a far greater extent than most people care to acknowledge. This control has nothing to do with the avoidance of all feelings. Rather, it is only effective when you *stop* avoiding them. Emotions can be welcomed, turned to your advantage, and used to enhance your life. The key, I believe, after you have learned how to become emotionally honest, lies in learning how to deal with one's thoughts.

I need to qualify what I have just written by drawing attention to one further common mistake that you can make regarding your emotions. If you believe that you are entirely responsible for everything you feel, you may be setting yourself up for emotional trouble. While this may be true up to a point, it is possible that many reading this book will occasionally experience emotional states for which they are not entirely responsible. Emotions, mainly the unpleasant ones, can be the result of disturbed body functioning. Glands may be oversecreting or undersecreting, or parts of the autonomic nervous system may be overreactive or underreactive—and these are hardly your fault. Particularly troublesome in this regard is the thyroid gland. When it is dysfunctional it can produce much emotional instability, with extreme mood swings occurring very suddenly. A high percentage of women clients I see in individual psychotherapy have some problem with the thyroid gland and are receiving treatment for this disorder. While many of the psychological problems they are experiencing are not directly attributable to this dysfunction, the frequency with which this problem occurs must highlight how our glands influence our emotions. If you are experiencing mood swings or emotional discomfort regularly, and there is no apparent reason for this, I would recommend that you go for a thorough medical evaluation. It is just possible that you are suffering from some physical disorder.

Common Misunderstandings About the Nature of Emotions

I find that many people (including those who claim to be Christians) believe a number of erroneous ideas about the nature of emotion. Holding on to these misconceptions can cause more problems than the emotions themselves, so I would like to comment on four of them, briefly:

"If I give in to my emotions, I will lose control of myself." The underlying fear here is that losing control of emotion is what causes insanity. This is just not true. Serious psychological disturbances are much more complex than this. If anything, quite the reverse is true. If you don't allow yourself to feel, you could be setting yourself up for emotional problems.

"I must never let my emotions get the better of me; if I do, I will be sinning." Emotions themselves are not sin. It's what we do with them that has the potential for becoming sin. Feelings or emotions are neither good nor bad in themselves. They are important signals that our bodies are sending us. We need to pay attention to these signals. If we train ourselves to avoid or ignore them altogether, we are missing an important aspect of our humanity and may be robbing ourselves of that which is uniquely ours as human beings, the highest of all God's creation. The ability to feel and emote and to integrate these into our experience is what separates us from the animal world. Emotions can bring us a better understanding of ourselves and thus enable us to live life more intelligently, as God intended it.

"As a Christian I should be free from emotional reaction. I should be calm at all times, never too high or too low." What a ridiculous idea! The outcome of this is that when our experience calls for an appropriate feeling, we lack the ability to feel appropriately. We can't love when we should, cry when we ought, or be joyful when our heaven opens to us! We become stunted, cold, distant, overcontrolled, and "blah" people. A woman came to me after a recent lecture I had given at a local church and told me

that every time she heard someone praying a beautiful prayer, she wanted to cry. She asked me what she could do about her problem. I was flabbergasted and obviously showed it. I asked her if she knew what her real problem was, and she quickly realized from the tone of my voice that she had an overconcern about what others would think of her. I told her that she could cry as often as she wanted to whenever anyone prayed, and I stood there with my own tears streaming down my face as I saw the relief that this advice brought to her. "Feel free to feel" is the essence of being emotionally real and healthy.

"Prayer alone can take away emotions that are out of control." I know many who feel that the only thing they can do whenever they are sad, depressed, hurt, upset, or angry is pray. When I ask them what they pray about, I invariably find that they pray about "the other person" or whatever is the *cause* of their feeling. "Please, God, take them away!" is the usual prayer. Seldom do they focus on themselves and the feelings they are experiencing at that moment. They won't recognize that their feelings are their own and that it is not necessary to wait until their circumstances change before attempting to change themselves.

The Joy of Emotional Freedom

We human beings are extremely complex emotional organisms. The extent of our emotions (and the way in which we cope with them) is probably what separates us most widely from the rest of creation. Animals cannot feel as we do. Their responses are conditioned responses more than they are the expressions of free, emoting creatures. Your dog may wag its tail as a sign of love to you, but the love you are capable of showing to others, as well as to the dog, far surpasses anything your pet has to offer. Your feelings do not have to be conditioned responses to what others have done for you, but have the capacity to be totally unconditional.

Through your emotions, you have the potential for deriving the greatest pleasure and joy which life has to offer. They provide the excitement and thrill of living that no other aspect of your being can provide. Take away your capacity to feel (as is done in certain forms of brain surgery) and life suddenly loses its luster. No longer can you feel the thrill of excitement, the flush of embarrassment, the sobering of a down feeling, and the happiness and joy of some new experience. Your feelings, both pleasant and unpleasant, give your life sparkle and should therefore be embraced, understood, and taken charge of in such a way that they are used to enhance your life.

On the other hand, your emotions have the ability to cause you the greatest misery that it is possible for a human being to suffer. Lose control of an unpleasant emotion such as depression and you will soon lose any reason for wanting to stay alive. This should not cause you to want to avoid your emotions, but rather motivate you to turn them to your good. God has given you the capacity for utilizing your complex emotional system for your benefit, and it should be a force that draws you nearer to Him and not, as it so often becomes, a means of self-destruction. To help you become emotionally free—to be able to experience your emotions in a healthy, positive, constructive way, and to turn and direct them with God's help towards making your life more abundant—will be my goal throughout this book.

Summary

There are two extremes of emotional experience, and both can produce an attitude to emotion that is destructive and self-defeating. Either we tend to allow our emotions to overwhelm us, and therefore come to fear them as if they were the enemy within, or we overcontrol them and rob ourselves of the many rich experiences they can bring. It requires effort to strike a balance between the two and know how to be free in the experiencing of one's emotions and how to make them work for you and bring happiness and enjoyment. It does not come naturally.

The problem of emotion is even more complex for Christians, who must contend with bringing the emotional side of their beings into harmony with their spiritual side. There are a number of common mistakes that are made by Christians, including the denial of feelings, succumbing to emotions in a defeatist way, and believing that we are totally responsible for everything we feel. A proper attitude toward emotions, with the recognition that they are God-given and intended to enhance our lives, can free us to experience them in a healthy way.

Additional Reading

1. *Emotional Common Sense: How to Avoid Self-Destructiveness.* Rolland S. Parker. New York: Harper & Row.
2. *The Art of Understanding Yourself.* Cecil Osborne. Grand Rapids, Michigan: Zondervan.
3. *The Doctor and the Soul: From Psychotherapy to Logotherapy.* Viktor E. Frankl. New York: Random House.
4. Romans 12.

2
Our Confusing Emotions

AS PSYCHOLOGISTS, we probably know less about emotion than about any other broad topic in the field of psychology. Indicative of the great complexity of the emotions is the considerable theorizing that has taken place about them over the years. We know more about learning, perception, development, and even the nature of personality, than we do about emotion. Descartes, who lived from 1596 to 1650, might just as well have written his *Passions of the Soul* in our day, for in it he states: "There is nothing in which the defective nature of the sciences which we have received from the ancients appears more clearly than in what they have written on the passions."

While our emotions may be as much of a mystery to ourselves as they are to the scientific psychological community, I don't mean to imply that we cannot avoid experiencing unpleasant and unwanted emotions and learn how to induce positive emotions. Acquiring this ability can radically change a personality and transform a life from being an unbearable chore to becoming a satisfying and deeply meaningful experience. To do this we must first come to grips with the confusing nature of our emotions and have a clear understanding of the many factors that produce our feelings.

We are complex emotional organisms, and many factors con-

26

tribute to our emotional states. We are also as distinctively different in the area of the emotions as we are with our fingerprints. Each of us is unique, and we produce our particular emotional patterns quite differently. If you are a male, you will not respond to the world in quite the same way as you would if you were a woman. Your age, the condition of your physical health, your personality, and a host of other factors will all have a major influence on how you experience your emotions.

Have you ever wondered whether the feeling of depression you experience is *exactly* the same as that experienced by some other person? How can you ever know? Unfortunately, you can't enter into another's experience and find out. All you have in order to equate your feeling experiences are the outward signs which show enough similarity to what you are experiencing for you to be able to identify and label them. No two people, however, ever experience *exactly* the same emotion. Each of us is unique, and each feeling we experience is *our own*.

The Complexity of Emotions

How many emotions are there? This question has always fascinated philosophers, poets, and psychologists. It cannot be answered as easily as you might suppose. One reason for this is that the terms used to describe emotion are often vague. Finding good technical terms for the various emotions has been extremely difficult, and this task has been magnified by the tendency for psychological traditions to perpetuate their biases. Another reason it has been difficult to establish a sound classification for the emotions is that they are themselves extremely complex. Take anger, for example. It is more a description of a whole variety of emotional reactions, rather than just one single type of experience. To fully describe a particular person's anger feeling you will have to take into account his age, the situation, preceding factors, and much more. To say that a child is angry is not the same as saying that an adult is angry. Animals certainly cannot be "angry" in the same way as we can. If there are that many aspects to anger, how is it possible to describe them completely by the single descriptive term of *anger?*

William James, one of psychology's giants, tried to come to

terms with the problem of emotion as early as 1884 when he published an article called "What Is Emotion?" He later proposed the idea that there were basically two levels of emotion. At the first level we have the "coarse" or fundamental type of emotion of which there are four: (1) grief; (2) fear; (3) rage; and (4) love. The second is a "fine" or subtle level of emotion which is derived from these four fundamental types.

While this theory would not receive acceptance in all psychological circles, it does have value in emphasizing a number of important points which can help us come to understand how our emotions work. Let me draw attention to just three:

1. If James's theory is correct, there is basically a very limited set of fundamental emotions from which we derive our many feelings. These variations on the primary emotional theme may be caused by situational factors, and this gives us the impression that we experience many more emotions than we really do.

2. It would be wrong to believe that there is no overlap between our emotions. There are no clear boundaries between one feeling and another, and it is possible, for example, to be feeling both angry and depressed at the same time and for these not to be separate feelings, but an amalgam of one feeling. This could have important implications for how you deal with your emotions, as there is in this instance only one and not two feelings to be dealt with.

3. Emotions are not simply "in your head." It is easy in this age, when everything is psychologized, to believe that emotions are purely psychological. Quite the contrary! We should always remember that our emotions involve a complex interaction between psychological and physiological factors and that we cannot separate the one from the other. True, it is often your thoughts, attitudes, and beliefs that trigger your emotional state, but emotion does not exist until some aspect of your physiology has been activated. Once the thought or idea has been removed, therefore, you must not expect your emotion to go away immediately. Depending on the severity and type of emotion, it may take a little while for your physiology to return to normal. This is often overlooked in the case of anger and depression.

Misconceptions About the Nature of Emotion

We are dogged by many misconceptions about the nature of emotion. We perpetuate these misconceptions without thinking about their full meanings and the implications they have for our mental health. This misunderstanding tends to create more problems than the emotions themselves, because it has such a powerful influence on our expectations and behavior. Take anger again as an example. One common misconception, unfortunately also held by many psychologists, is that anger can be stored up—and if it is not released periodically, it will cause us some mental harm. This idea treats anger as an entity, an energy of some sort, which can be accumulated. It furthermore leads us to believe that we can do nothing to stop the process and that once the anger tank has been filled it *must* be drained off. I will discuss this misconception in more detail in chapter 5, but let me ask at this stage that if it is possible for anger to be stored up in this way, why do we not also store up love, joy, envy, fear, and so on? These emotions simply do not accumulate—because they do not exist as single entities. They are the final product of complex interactions between our minds and our bodies. The variety of these combinations is infinite, and this is probably why the poets have done a better job of describing the emotions than have scientifically trained psychologists. Perhaps poets know how to put feelings into their situational and personality contexts and thus are better able to capture and describe the true essence of our emotions.

Other misconceptions about the nature of emotion which are commonly held by Christians are:

1. A Christian should never be subject to extremes of emotional reaction.
2. It is sin that causes emotional disorders.
3. Our parents are to blame for all our emotional hang-ups.

These ideas are patently ridiculous and yet are held by many to be true, consequently causing unnecessary guilt and suffering. Being a Christian does not stop us from being human and from being subject to those emotions which are the normal response to life's experiences. True, Christians have resources available to deal with many of life's problems, but they should not expect to be completely devoid of feeling. Emotions are God-given and inherently good for us. Something has gone wrong when we allow them to become destructive.

Feelings Versus Emotions

Up to this point I have used the terms *feelings* and *emotions* interchangeably. To be technically correct, we should distinguish between them, as they do have slightly different meanings. Feelings are basically an essential part of what is meant by emotion. They are the part of emotion which breaks through into our awareness. A feeling is the sensation or bodily state that accompanies the experience of the emotion. Feeling depends on our interest and attention at the moment of experiencing the emotion. If we are not attending to our emotion, we may not *feel* anything. On the other hand, emotion refers to the deeper, underlying state that stirs or agitates us, whether or not we are aware of it as feeling. When we experience the emotion, when our senses tell us that something is alerting or agitating us, we have a feeling state.

It is unfortunate that we have also come to use the term *feel* to describe purposes other than those describing the emotions. We "feel" with our hands. We even "feel" with our intellect, as when we say, "I feel that you have as much right to sit by the window as he does." It is not surprising to find that this multiple use of the word *feel* has contaminated our understanding of how to experience feelings. We often shortchange ourselves in experiencing our emotions because we don't really understand the difference between the true feeling of an emotion and the many other things we feel. This may cause some people, especially men, to engage in intellectualizing and yet think they are feeling.

Emotional Chaining

One very important point to remember about your emotions is that they are not always an end in themselves. One emotion can be the cause of another emotion, just like an echo can cause a further echo. The sound of an echo keeps bouncing backwards and forwards between mountain surfaces until it finally dies out by losing energy. Similarly, you can react to an emotion within yourself and develop another emotion, and this second emotion can create a third, and so on. Fortunately, the process weakens in most cases and eventually dies because of lack of energy. Sometimes, however, it does not weaken and there can easily be an escalation in the severity of an emotion until something serious happens. I call this "emotional chaining," and it is an extremely important principle that must be understood if you are going to develop a healthy way for controlling your emotions.

As an example of how emotional chaining can take place, let us suppose that you have become depressed over the loss of your job. Such a loss generally creates feelings of frustation, since the loss represents a major obstacle to the achievement of the goals you have for your life. When you are frustrated, you are extremely anger prone and may find some way to express your anger, such as writing a nasty letter to your immediate supervisor or blaming someone else for the job loss. As soon as you realize that you have become angry, you may experience an intensification of your depression because you feel that you are not in control of yourself. More depression may mean more anger—and the cycle can repeat itself over and over again until your depression reaches serious proportions.

If you pause for a moment, you will not find it difficult to remember examples from your own life of how one emotion created another in a chaining pattern. The disappointment of some expectation can cause you to develop hate feelings toward the one who has disappointed you. Embarrassment can give rise to self-hate and self-rejection. Jealousy can cause the most intense anxiety feelings.

I knew one person who was very prone to this chaining pattern, and it nearly caused her to lose her life. In a fit of anger one day she walked out of her home with the intention of moving in with a friend on the other side of the city. Deep down in her fantasy, she was expecting her husband to follow after her, find her, and then plead with her to come back home after declaring his error and begging for forgiveness. No sooner had she left her home, however, than a deep sense of embarrassment came over her for her uncontrollable anger, and this sense of loss (which was really a loss of self-esteem) triggered a severe depressive reaction. She felt that she could not again face herself—let alone her family—for doing this, so she decided that the only thing she could do was to take her own life with an overdose of sleeping pills. Fortunately, the attempt failed, and nothing more than a sore stomach was the consequence.

The reason we have the ability to chain from one emotion to another is that we engage in reflecting upon and evaluating our emotions. We tend to want to label our emotions as "good" or "bad," and this causes us to react with further emotions, depending on how we value them. We fear and want to avoid certain emotions. We are certainly not proud of ourselves for being angry or jealous and always want to feel that we are in complete control of ourselves. We don't enjoy embarrassment or making mistakes, so that when we experience these feelings we react with fear or disgust and thus create a new emotion. This new emotion is often more intense and disastrous than the original.

What can we do about this? The first step is to come to know yourself well enough that you can recognize whether or not you are chaining your emotions. Your past experiences can tell you whether you are prone to this. Examine the expectations you have of yourself and see whether they are not too idealistic and demanding. Do you, for example, expect never to fail? This is unrealistic and irrational. Whatever else you might believe about yourself, you need to remember that you are only human and therefore need to make room in your life for occasional failures. Try to develop an attitude which says to yourself, "Failures are to grow by!" Examine the fears you have of your emotions: Where do they come from? Do you need to be so afraid of them? By facing these fears openly and honestly, you can reduce their power to create unpleasant reactions to your emotions. Once you have developed some ability to stop creating new emotions out of existing ones, your battle is half over, since you are then free to focus your attention on the original emotion and take the steps necessary to deal with it.

Psychotherapy and Emotion

From my discussion so far, you should be able to see why it is so difficult for people to get in touch with their emotions. It is possible for emotions to exist for a long time without ever becoming feelings which can be identified and acknowledged. We human beings have a remarkable ability to avoid attending to our emotions, and consequently it is possible to be totally ignorant of what is going on inside of ourselves. This is not true of people in all cultures. Some cultures teach their members to express their emotions much more readily than we do, and consequently these people are not as afraid as we are to show their feelings. They may shout a lot and engage in a variety of histrionics, but they show their affection easily and are not afraid to be labeled as emotional. The remarkable consequence of this cultural style is that there appears to be a much lower incidence of the neurotic disorders. Psychiatrists and psychologists are jokingly described as finding it hard to make a living in these cultures.

This raises a very important but vexed question. Given the emotionally restrictive nature of our culture, what are we supposed to do with our feelings? We cannot suddenly change our cultural patterns, and the advice we receive from popular books and magazine articles only increases our confusion. We are told to "release" our emotions. This idea is grossly misleading. It implies that something is dammed up inside which must be drained away. Since emotions are experiences which involve every part of one's being, how can we release them? Another misleading expression that is often bandied about is to "look at" our emotions. There is nothing to look at. Emotions are dispersed throughout one's whole being—like salt dissolved in a glass of water. How could we possibly look at the salt? Emotions can be felt, experienced, and reflected upon, but never seen. What, then, are we to do with them?

We may get some help here if we take a moment to examine what psychotherapists do when they work with a client's emotions. While therapeutic styles differ greatly, there are some common features in all psychotherapy. What are they?

Psychotherapists explore the events that precede an emotional experience. To be able to identify all the factors that precede an emotional experience is extremely important in coming to understand the emotion. Unfortunately, the one experienc-

ing the emotion may frequently be so taken up with how he is
feeling that he fails to fully realize what it was that caused the
feeling. Often the real cause is not the one that is presented by the
client, and consequently the emotion does not subside when steps
are taken to deal with the supposed cause. Therefore, the
psychotherapist helps to identify the real cause of the emotion. A
husband may suddenly find himself depressed. At first he does not
know why he is depressed, but then his wife comes to him with
the monthly bills and reminds him that they have not yet caught
up with their Christmas expenses. He immediately launches into
an attack on her, accusing her of being a loose spender and having
no consideration for how hard he works. Implied in this attack is
his belief that his wife is the cause of his depression, when in
actuality he has only just found a convenient excuse for his depression. The real cause may lie in some recent event in his work
situation that he was not owning up to. Of course, it is possible for
multiple causes to lie behind our emotions, and we cannot always
precisely determine the factors involved. Sometimes it is sufficient merely to eliminate the more obvious ones and thus relieve
our friends, spouses, and children of any responsibility for how we
feel.

***Psychotherapists increase the person's awareness of emo-
tion.*** Emotions have the remarkable ability to exist and yet
elude our awareness and attention. In psychotherapy, we help
individuals to become more aware of emotions by focusing attention on what they are feeling from time to time. Often we will stop
and ask a client, "What are you feeling at this moment?" By so
doing, we train the client to monitor what he is feeling. But a
person who cannot understand his or her problems may only be
further confused by being made aware of the underlying feelings.
The purpose of increasing someone's awareness of feeling is to
force him to identify and face the real problem. A client may
previously have avoided recognizing or wanting to talk about the
real problem. By increasing awareness of feelings, and even allowing him to become angry or cry, the therapist is moving the
client toward a place of courage and willingness to face the real
problem.

Psychotherapists clarify the nature of a person's emotion. As therapists, we encourage clients to "taste" rather than "look at" emotion. Often this involves helping clients to build a feeling vocabulary, so that they can more accurately describe what they are experiencing. Our language is notably deficient when it comes to expressing feelings, and this is one of the reasons why we find it so satisfying to use verbal obscenities. Swearwords, because they often do not have any precise definition, can take on many different meanings and this, combined with their shock value, can serve to provide a release for our feelings which is quite unique. It is not my aim to advocate swearing as a healthy outlet for expressing feelings. I am only trying to point out that, by helping clients to accurately label and describe how and what they are feeling, we can provide both understanding of the problems and clarification of the corrective steps that need to be taken in order to resolve them. This is quite different from the idea of "releasing" your emotions by, for example, allowing yourself to cry or become angry. Under some conditions this can be helpful, but doing this over and over again may never solve any of your problems. You may, in fact, find yourself becoming a more and more angry person or tending to cry much more easily. The clarification of your emotions which comes from accurately labeling them can help you come to a better understanding of what *causes* them.

Psychotherapists facilitate the experience of emotion. Spending one's life overcontrolling and suppressing emotion can use up a lot of energy. A person who lives this way is very prone to develop a neurotic life-style. Often this overcontrol generalizes to all the emotions, so that if we cannot allow ourselves to feel angry, we also won't allow ourselves to love or be loved. It is very difficult to train ourselves in controlling only one emotion while letting all the other emotions have their freedom. Thus, as therapists we may take "tasting" a step further and encourage someone to experience an emotion very deeply. A client is only able to do this when he has much trust and confidence in the therapist. I recently had as a client a fifty-year-old woman whose husband had been killed in an automobile accident five years before. When I first saw her she was complaining of insomnia, headaches, and general tension. As we explored her problem, it became obvious that she had never recovered from her husband's death. Life had come to a standstill for her, primarily because she had not completed her grieving over the loss. My therapy focused on helping her experience her grief as deeply as possible. This was painful for both of us, but gradually, out of this experiencing of her grief at a deep level, she began to pull her life together again.

Psychotherapists encourage a more open expression of appropriate emotion. An emotionally "real" or healthy person is someone who knows what causes his or her emotions; can attend to, identify, and describe them; and is free to experience them to an appropriate degree. If our culture is at fault for training us to overcontrol our emotions, obviously we need to move ourselves to a more free experience and expression of them. Unfortunately for many, the only safe place that this can be done is in the trusting, confidential, and professional nature of a therapeutic relationship. Where else can you be yourself so completely? Nowhere, unfortunately. It is a sad thought to me that we who profess to have received unconditional grace from our Creator should find it so hard to show the same grace to our fellow creatures in giving them total acceptance. Love is something we talk a lot about in Christian circles, but have a long way to go in demonstrating. Our attitude to emotional experiences and the taboos we place on their expression are major factors in preventing us from fully experiencing love in our Christian communities.

Fortunately, there is one other place where you can be yourself totally and completely and have the freedom to express your emotions unreservedly. It is the place of prayer! No doubt many of you have found this to be the most therapeutic of all experiences. I never cease to marvel at what I know can happen there!

Our Many Selves

One of the biggest mistakes you can make in trying to understand your emotions is to divide yourself up into "life compartments," and then to see yourself as being made up of these separate compartments. You may see yourself as having an intellec-

tual compartment, a physical compartment, a reasoning compartment, and so on. Nowhere is this idea more misleading than
in the area of your emotions. Just as there are many aspects to
your total being, there are also many aspects to your emotions,
and you should constantly remind yourself that you do not function as dismembered compartments but as a totally integrated
being. It is artificial to separate your mind from your body, your
emotions from your thoughts, or your actions from your intentions. As the Gestalt psychologists would say, "The whole is more
than the sum of its parts," and this applies as much to your emotions as it does to anything else. There can only be value in examining the parts of your being if you don't make the mistake of
seeing these parts in isolation from one another.

One common way in which we compartmentalize ourselves is to
separate the psychological aspects of our beings from the
physiological. As Christian believers we would probably want to
make this a three-part compartment and also add our spiritual
aspect. This compartmentalization extends even to the health-
care services, where we have established separate professions for
taking care of the psychological, the physiological, and the
spiritual needs of humankind. While some effort has been made
to restore the whole by emphasizing the interactive aspect of
these compartments—for example, through the psychosomatic-
medicine emphasis—the average layperson still tends to think of
himself (or herself) in terms of clearly separate aspects of being.

But why is this an important issue? Mainly because it is very
common to find that people do not make allowance for the fact
that physiological factors can play an important role in influencing emotional conditions—and vice versa. We could also say that
spiritual conditions can influence both physiological and
psychological states—and vice versa. I certainly know that when
I am fatigued, both my psychological and spiritual well-being are
affected. To be emotionally healthy we must be sensitive to these
interactive factors.

I have, for example, had a number of clients who have presented themselves with the complaint that they frequently experience periods of depression. As I have examined their life-
styles, habits, and so on, I have found that they are invariably

overworked, eat poorly, don't know how to relax, and are caught up in a constant round of having to please everybody they encounter. They complain of always feeling fatigued and never take time for recreation. The interesting thing is that seldom do they realize that there is a connection between their fatigue and their depression. After providing them with some help in rearranging the priorities in their lives, teaching them how to relax effectively and making sure they eat well-balanced meals, I have learned that their depression diminished dramatically. Of course, not all depression will go away just because you do these things, but it is important to realize that your physiology is an essential part of your emotional makeup, and if you disturb or abuse your physiology, you will pay for it with emotional disturbances. It does not take a genius to see where the problem must be tackled.

The danger of ignoring obvious physiological factors in emotion.   Some physiological disturbances, however, are more permanent in their effects and much more difficult to correct. The consequences of some diseases or brain states are not that easy to predict, nor do you know all the causes of some emotional disturbances. There is a form of depression, for example, that is described as "endogenous," meaning that it comes from within your body. It is not related to any way to obvious environmental factors, as no identifiable precipitating event can be located—and there is strong evidence to support the idea that it is caused by some biochemical disturbance in the body. Those who suffer from this disorder do so for many years without seeking appropriate help, or when it is offered they refuse to take it, simply because they don't understand that the real cause is in their physiological makeup.

What happens if we do not make allowance for these physiological factors? We tend to look in the wrong places for the reasons for our unpleasant emotional states. We look around in our environment for factors to blame, and if our husbands or wives, our children, our employers, our friends, or even our pets are conveniently available, we may place the blame on them. In blaming them, we inappropriately set the stage for further disturbances. Those we blame may feel unjustly accused and may engage in a counterattack in order to defend themselves.

A good example of this occurred with a married couple I once worked with a few years ago. Ever since they were first married they have caused each other considerable emotional pain, despite the fact that they love each other dearly. The husband was depression prone (of the endogenous variety I have described above). Every time he felt "down" (averaging about once every two or three weeks), he would blame his wife for his depression. Since she was only human, he did not have great difficulty in finding something that he could blame. She would become upset at his accusations and would defensively pull away from him and refuse to talk. He would then experience further depression as a response to this loss and would intensify his attacks on her. After many days of misery, the depression would finally go away, and they would make up—only to have the cycle repeat itself again after a few weeks, with enough variety for the obviousness of the cycle to elude their attention. The saddest part of all was that they claimed to be Christians, and the turmoil of their marriage had caused so much havoc in their spiritual lives that they were on the point of giving that up also. When they finally came to see me about their problem, I referred the husband for appropriate medication to stabilize his endogenous depression and taught him through psychotherapy how to deal more directly with his depression proneness. He quickly learned how to stop blaming his environment for his depression, and their marriage began to mend.

In another case, the wife was clearly at fault. She experienced periods of emotional disturbance that resulted in uncontrolled episodes of confusion. She put the blame for this on her husband until their first child was born and then blamed both the husband and the child. Even when she was separated from her spouse (as occurred when she had to be left at home alone due to the nature of his work), she continued to blame him. At first the husband believed she was right and tried everything to placate her. Eventually he became exasperated, realized that he was not entirely responsible for her feelings, and demanded that they seek professional help. Unfortunately, the wife was not very responsive to therapy and refused to undergo an appropriate evaluation for the causes of her confusion states, and their marriage eventually broke up. Such an unhappy outcome is most unfortunate, especially since I was convinced that her problem was physical in nature and could be easily corrected by treatment.

Summary

Our emotions are extremely complex. As a result they are confusing both to ourselves and to the scientific community. While we seem, as human beings, to be capable of a wide variety of emotional experiences, they are probably based on only a relatively few basic emotions.

Misconceptions about the nature of emotion abound, and they tend to create more problems than the emotions themselves. It is important, therefore, that we have a clear understanding of what causes and what perpetuates our emotions.

Chaining of emotions—where one emotion gives rise to a second as a reaction to it—can not only make it difficult to identify the original problem, but can keep us in a perpetual state of confusion. Learning to stop doing this requires that you not continually label what you are feeling as "good" or "bad." If you are feeling something, go ahead and feel it. Give yourself permission to do this and you will not react with further anger, depression, or self-condemnation.

What happens in psychotherapy, as we learn how to become freer and more accepting of emotions (particularly the unpleasant ones), is a good model of what we should be doing in our daily lives. This means training ourselves to explore the events that precede an emotional experience, increasing our awareness of emotion, clarifying our emotions, and being more open to experiencing feelings.

Additional Reading

1. *Our Many Selves*. Elizabeth O'Connor. New York: Harper & Row.
2. *The Kink and I: A Psychiatrist's Guide to Untwisted Living*. James D. Mallory and Stanley Baldwin. Wheaton, Illinois: Victor Books.

3. *The Christian and Mental Health.* Samuel Southard. Nashville: Broadman.
4. *The Experience of Psychotherapy: What It's Like for Client and Therapist.* William H. Fitts. New York: Van Nos Reinhold.
5. Romans 6.

3

How Thoughts Cause Emotions

IT IS DR. ALBERT ELLIS who stresses that human beings seem
to have a natural tendency to think crookedly and therefore easily establish and maintain self-defeating patterns of behavior and
emotion. By "crooked thinking" he means the tendency to think
irrationally or to hold on to the most ridiculous beliefs, despite
evidence to the contrary. This tendency to think irrationally,
Ellis contends, is a major cause for what we experience as
neurosis. More importantly for our purpose, he would contend
that it is a major factor in causing many of the emotional upsets
we experience. I don't agree with everything Dr. Ellis says, but I
do agree on these points at least, and the purpose of this chapter is
to show that even if we are Christian believers, we are not im-
mune to this tendency to think crookedly and believe the most
ridiculous ideas. We can have as much crooked thinking in our
Christian belief systems as we can in any other area of our lives.
This is not the fault of the basic truths of the Gospel which, in my
opinion, are healthy and health producing. But most of us have
derived our beliefs from secondhand sources and have consequently assimilated all the distortions of those who have ever
influenced us.

The Confusion in Psychology

We have recently come through a period of great confusion in some schools of psychology about how to handle our emotions. There has been far too much preoccupation with the feelings themselves and not enough emphasis placed on the importance of recognizing what *causes* feelings. While there is therapeutic value in expressing and experiencing one's emotions (and this is certainly an essential part of being emotionally healthy), the feeling or emotion itself is only the end product of a chain of events. If one is to learn how to avoid an unpleasant emotion, it is necessary to look at the events that *precede* the emotion. This is what the cognitive theories of psychology emphasize. As a group, cognitive therapists are growing in number, and what they emphasize is that emotionally disturbed persons are not victimized by concealed forces that are beyond their awareness and over which they have no control. Emotions are neither mysterious nor impossible to control, but can be explored and understood in the context of one's learning history and current patterns of thinking.

This approach has great appeal to me, not only because it provides me with a powerful and effective therapeutic tool, but because I can see in it important concepts for integrating theology and psychology. The Gospel places tremendous importance on beliefs and their power to shape one's life. Of course, it is not merely the nature of belief per se that is important, but also the truthfulness of the content of the belief. When one believes a set of truths as powerful as those contained in the Christian Gospel, one is at least shaping many powerful beliefs about human nature, love, forgiveness, and hope—which must have an effect on our emotions.

As a Man Thinketh

James Allen wrote a wonderful little book called *As a Man Thinketh,* in which he says (springing off Proverbs 23:7): "A man is literally what he thinks, his character being the complete sum of all his thoughts."

I would take this idea further and reword what Allen says as follows: "People feel what they think. Their emotions are the complete sum of all their thoughts." I am sure that James Allen would agree with me if he were alive today, based on what he has to say in the rest of his book. He was born in 1864 and died in 1912, but in this little book he was able to describe much of what would become our modern approach to cognitive therapeutic psychology. Listen to what he has to say: "The body is the servant of the mind. It obeys the operations of the mind, whether they be deliberately chosen or automatically expressed. At the bidding of unlawful thoughts the body sinks rapidly into disease and decay; at the command of glad and beautiful thoughts it becomes clothed with youthfulness and beauty."

If we substitute *irrational* for "unlawful," *emotion* for "body," and *misery and unhappiness* for "disease and decay," no cognitive therapist could have said it better. The thoughts of our minds determine whether we will be happy or miserable, successful or a failure, composed or angry, relaxed or tense. Except for the rare occurrence of psychosis or the consequence of brain damage or obvious physiological disturbances, we must accept responsibility for the way we emote. While biological and environmental factors may interact to have an influence on our emotions, the fact remains that we have the capacity to intervene significantly between the environmental input and the emotional output in nearly all instances. If I did not believe this, I would not do psychotherapy. Potentially, at least, we have an enormous amount of control that we can exercise over what we feel and do. The real problem is that we lack the motivation and understanding to intervene. Most times when I have failed in my psychotherapy with someone, it has been due to the client's unwillingness to make any further effort to change. The advantages of changing were no longer paying a bigger dividend than the present self-defeating behaviors.

The Importance of Thoughts in Producing Emotions

Thoughts are important in influencing our emotions primarily because they give meaning to the events that occur to us. Thoughts in turn are influenced by our beliefs, attitudes, expectations, assumptions and perceptions, and before discussing these in more detail let me outline the chain of reaction which leads up to an unpleasant emotion. The most common understanding of what happens is as follows:

EVENT → (produces) → EMOTION

An example would be: A woman's husband criticizes her in front of her friends (EVENT) and this causes her to become so angry that she cannot talk the rest of the evening (EMOTION). This woman believes that the emotion was the direct consequence of the preceding event. In rational-emotive therapy (a form of cognitive therapy which Dr. Ellis has developed), the cause of the emotions would be labeled the "activating" event (A) and the final emotion as the "consequence" (C). Thus A causes or leads to C. This idea is so commonly held and so infrequently challenged that many assume it to be a natural law.

The essence of the cognitive approach is to emphasize that between the A and the C there is an intervening B, namely the "belief system" of the individual. Thus, A can only cause C through B, hence the A-B-C approach to understanding many emotions. What happens is more like the following:

EVENT   →   MEANING   →   EMOTION
(Activator)   (Belief System)   (Consequence)

It is the intermediate belief system that gives meaning to the event, and the emotion is a consequence of this meaning and *not* of the event.

For example, the woman whose husband criticizes her in front of her friends becomes angry only because her intervening belief system gives some meaning to the event. It mediates between the event and the consequence and is the *primary* cause of the consequence. True, it may all happen in a split second of time, and she may not need in this instance to think much about the event, but the consequence is nevertheless the product of her belief system. She may interpret the event as rejection; she may fear that her friends will believe what the husband is saying; she may not want to face up to her own inadequacies; or she may simply fear that this criticism will ultimately lead to rejection. These are all *belief* issues and are only secondarily related to the primary event.

While this can happen very rapidly, there may be times when we have ample opportunity to think about an event. The emotional consequence does not occur immediately but follows our mulling over the event and engaging in a lot of self-talk: "What did she mean when she said that?" "What was he hiding from me when he told me why he was late?" We muse and search our belief systems through the medium of thought, and then come up with an appropriate emotional reaction. Unfortunately, most times it is an unpleasant emotion. The influence of our beliefs on our emotions was even understood by Marcus Aurelius (A.D. 121–180) who said in *The Meditations:* "If you are pained by an external thing it is not this thing that disturbs you—but your judgment about it."

Emotions Can Be Changed

The most important implication of all of this is that our emotional reactions are *not* permanent parts of our personality but rather emerge out of the way we see ourselves, others, and God. Our beliefs, ideas, and attitudes determine our emotional reactions in pretty much the same way as a rudder determines the direction a boat will sail. True, the wind (our environment) and the ocean currents (our biology) may have something to say about the overall direction, but they can only interact with our rudders (beliefs) to produce the final outcome. If our rudders are used properly, they can, in fact, be used to transform the negative influences of the wind and current into an advantage. All it takes is a little effort at first, and it soon becomes a natural process. If you are criticized, you can turn that criticism to your advantage by using your intermediate thoughts. By remaining objective and rational, you can examine the criticism to see where it is justified—and by taking appropriate steps to rectify those defects that are true, you can then actually grow through the experience. Those elements of the criticism that are not true can be discarded in such a way that there can now be an extra freedom in your life as you need no longer fear those elements of the criticism that would immobilize you. Let me quote James Allen again on this point:

> A noble and Godlike character is not a thing of favor or chance, but is the *natural* result of *continued effort* in right thinking . . . he is the maker of his character, the molder of his life, and the builder of his destiny, if he will watch, con-

trol, and alter his thoughts, tracing their effects upon himself, upon others, and upon his life and circumstances.

How Are Thoughts Formed?

In our waking moments we are bombarded by a stream of thoughts. These thoughts are influenced by what is going on around us as well as what is happening *inside* us. If you are driving on the freeway, having just come from an important business meeting and having not yet eaten lunch, your thoughts are likely to be switching from the events of the meeting, to the cars and people on the freeway, to lunch, and then back to the others. You may also be anticipating activities for the afternoon. This type of thought stream is with you at all times. You may occasionally pause to reflect on its content, but if I were to take some physiological measures of your heart rate, respiration, and sweat-gland activity, I would be able to see a very direct representation of this stream of thought as it has a continuous influence on your body. It may speed up your heart, then slow it down. Constantly you are being prepared for action and then calmed down again, all under the influence of your thoughts. Your ability to handle stress is very much dependent on the reactivity of your physiological system to this stream of thought.

Overall, these thoughts are determined and greatly influenced by your beliefs, attitudes, expectations, assumptions, and perceptions. Either singly or in combination, these influences will determine the meanings that events have for you—in those split-second moments after something has happened or in the slower musings and thought processes which will follow activating events. Let us examine each of these in turn and see how they operate to affect your thoughts and hence your emotions.

BELIEFS reflect the acceptance of something as true. For example, in theology a belief is the firm persuasion of the truths of a religion. Our beliefs are formed and shaped by a number of factors. One such powerful influence is experience. We believe that airplanes can fly because we have seen and experienced their flying. I doubt if anything could shake this belief. We also believe that men have walked on the moon, although we have only seen pictures to prove this. The day that it was announced that the

United States had placed a man on the moon, I was talking to a primitive African woman in South Africa. She was illiterate and very cautious and told me that she only believed what she could see with her own eyes. I asked her if she knew that a man had stepped onto the moon just a few hours before. She thought I was joking. How could anyone believe such a thing!

"Have you seen it?" she asked me.

"No," I replied, "I only heard it announced on the radio." I don't mind confessing that I felt a little sheepish at her challenge. But if at that moment some action was called for which depended on that belief, I would have responded to it while the old woman would not. We had different beliefs, formed by our different experiences.

But not all our beliefs are formed by experience. Some beliefs are deeply ingrained in our minds, and we don't have a shred of evidence to support them—beliefs about the world, ourselves, the future, the past. Some beliefs are concrete while others are very abstract. I may believe that (1) when my car's tires are worn down to a certain level, I run a high risk of having an accident in wet weather; or (2) unless I am outstandingly competent and never fail in any project I undertake, I will not be accepted by my friends. The first belief is "rational," since there is evidence to support it; but the second is an example of what Albert Ellis calls "irrational," as there is not a shred of evidence to support the idea that my friends only care for me because I am competent. These terms are used rather loosely, but generally contrast those beliefs that can be empirically demonstrated (rational) with those that have no substantiation whatsoever (irrational). Whenever we invoke absolute terms such as "I've got to!" "I must!" or "I ought!" we are invariably invoking irrational ideas. These irrational beliefs give rise to irrational thoughts which are then followed by illogical thinking on deeply personal matters.

To illustrate these points: Being short, bald, or having a long nose is not really a problem in itself. It is clearly irrational to believe that because you have one (or all) of these defects you are not acceptable to others. There is no law or principle which says this must be so. If your belief about such attributes has become so distorted that their importance has become exaggerated, you are bound to develop a psychological problem or have emotional disturbances.

It is remarkable how many irrational ideas most of us carry around in our heads and how resistant they are to extinction. Of course, many of these distorted beliefs are acquired in childhood, but we then perpetuate them throughout our lives by failing to challenge them. We are often only aware of these irrational beliefs after we have suffered from their consequences, and seldom can we verbalize the idea or belief before it gets us into trouble.

Some of the irrational ideas we hold are quite universal in character. Dr. Ellis has identified many of those commonly found in emotionally disturbed people (and probably present to some lesser extent in all of us). If we hold to any of the following beliefs we are clearly crossing the boundary from rational to irrational:

- I must be loved and liked by everyone.
- I must be loved at all times, without exception.
- I must be perfectly competent in all that I do, if I am to be liked by my friends.
- I must never fail.
- I have no control over my own happiness.
- Everything bad that happens to me is catastrophic.
- Everyone must treat me fairly.
- I must experience pleasure rather than pain in my life.

The irrational flavor of these ideas will become patently obvious as you think about them. They are based on absolutes (no exceptions, blacks and whites rather than grays) and expectations way beyond what can be reasonably expected from human beings. These and similar irrational ideas, to the extent that they are believed and held below the conscious awareness of the individual, can lead to many negative emotions. It has been demonstrated over and over again (and I have experienced this in my own therapy with clients as well as in my personal life) that when a person—

- deliberately confronts and examines the ridiculous nature of these ideas . . .
- stops expecting their fulfillment . . .

- stops condemning himself for his own humanness and inability to meet all the expectations that others place on him . . .
- realizes at the deepest level of his being that God accepts him in Christ just as he is . . .
- stops judging himself and others for being human (which is God's prerogative) and . . .
- utilizes the resources of the Gospel to help him do all this . . .

he can practically eliminate most of the more serious and unwanted, unpleasant emotions. Does such a claim sound too strong? If it does, I apologize for making it sound that way. The positive nature of this statement is a reflection of my strong conviction of its truth, based on my experience as a psychotherapist.

ATTITUDES are also important in the formation of your thoughts and in influencing your emotions. By "attitude" is meant the disposition or tendency to respond in a particular way to people or objects. Attitudes can have their origins in our beliefs or they can be completely independent of them (or at least appear to be).

Some attitudes have the ability to create in us those split-second-response emotions which follow an event and therefore have tremendous power to disturb us. We have learned from past experience how to respond, without any apparent thinking, to people or objects in either a positive or a negative way. A prejudice is a biased attitude usually learned through imitation and involving emotional rejection and hostility. We all have attitudes and biases, but few are aware of them or take the trouble to become aware of them. If you are a typical middle-aged person staying in a holiday-resort hotel and a group of young people move into rooms on the same floor, it is highly possible that you will immediately react to their presence without even thinking, with some feelings of disappointment and fear that your comfort and sleep will be disturbed. This will probably spoil the rest of your day, if not the rest of your vacation. What has happened? Something triggered your prejudices about young people, and your attitude toward them was then determined. You do not know when you first see them whether they are well-behaved or rowdy, and you probably did not even stop to think about it. Your feelings were triggered automatically. The same would be true if you had intruded on a group of young people. Their attitudes to you would have been determined by their prejudices.

Changing attitudes is a very complex task, and in this short review on how our thinking influences our emotions I could not possibly provide you with a comprehensive set of guidelines. What I can say is that you can go a long way toward reducing your prejudices and ensuring healthy attitudes by—

- openly admitting that you are subject to many prejudices (since we are all safe in admitting this) . . .
- being on guard against negative attitudes . . .
- stopping yourself as soon as you become aware of the attitude or prejudice that is triggering your emotion and . . .
- challenging it with all your mental ability and forcing yourself to see the other side of the issue and identify the reasons for your reaction.

Let me illustrate this with the example I gave earlier. You are the middle-aged person enjoying your vacation at a seaside resort. You notice that a group of young people has just arrived and occupied rooms close to you. Becoming annoyed and even angry, you say to yourself, "Now I will never get any sleep! I have paid all this money only to get a bunch of rowdy kids in my hair." You stop yourself and admit that your attitude to young people has been prejudiced from past experience.

"Need I get angry?" you ask yourself. "It's not going to chase them away. How do I know that they will be rowdy? I have no evidence for that. Perhaps I am only envious of their youth and jealous of their ability to have fun so easily and freely. If they disturb my sleep, I will ask them nicely to be considerate of my needs. In the meantime, if I am nice to them instead of being angry, I will achieve two things: I will recapture some of my lost youth and get some vicarious satisfaction from being around some fun; I will win them as my friends, so that if I have to ask them to be considerate, they will be only too happy to oblige such 'nice people.' "

Perhaps at this point you will have noticed that your emotional *pain* had become emotional *pleasure*. Is this difficult to achieve?

Only if you do not want to take the time to watch, control, and alter your attitudes—and if you prefer emotional pain to emotional pleasure.

Notice one very important aspect of this technique. What we say to ourselves, our self-talk, plays a major role in influencing our emotions once they have been triggered. Your initial anger could be intensified if you had begun to say, "I should never have come to this place. Everything always works against me . . . ." If we control our self-talk and begin to think and talk more rationally and objectively, we can do a turnabout in our emotions. Obviously, this takes some practice and the investment of a little effort. Unfortunately, it seems to be so much easier for us to go with the negative thoughts and self-talk, almost as if we prefer to be miserable rather than happy. As self-talk is so important to emotional happiness, I will devote a special section to it toward the end of this chapter.

EXPECTATIONS: "He always comes home from work, goes straight to his favorite chair, and opens the newspaper. He never comes and kisses me first, and I do not like that."

"Why," I ask my client who has tears streaming down her face at this point, "do you continue to make yourself miserable by expecting your husband to be different? He has never come home from work and kissed you as his first act, so what makes you think he is going to be any different the next time?"

This sort of conversation occurs regularly in my therapy with clients. If it's not about spouses, it concerns children, bosses, and even pets! We set ourselves up for depression, for anger, for rejection, and for defeat by convincing ourselves that we have a right to expect something. That something can be love, respect, consideration, and many others. We build up a hope that something will happen at a certain time (with very little real cause to expect it), and when it doesn't happen we experience an emotional disappointment. This can happen over and over again, and we seldom recognize the pattern.

When my wife and I first came to California, I found a piece of acreage that I fell in love with. It had a magnificent view and there was a FOR SALE sign on it. My fantasy ran wild. I imagined myself as the owner of the property and built up my expectations for obtaining it. We contacted the real-estate agent whose name was on the board, and he thought I could get it for a reasonable price. My expectations ran higher. My hopes filled out like a hot-air balloon and soared away on the winds of my imagination. And then the blow came. "I'm sorry, Doctor Hart, but the owner tells me that he does not want to sell the land anymore!" was the realtor's disappointing message. I had failed to keep my expectations within reasonable limits, and the loss I experienced was as devastating to me as if I had actually lost my own land.

There are many instances in life where we create unreasonable expectations in our minds. Since they are unreasonable and are very seldom satisfied, we experience many letdowns and the consequent unpleasant emotional reactions. We anticipate some gift or build up our expectations for some event, and when it doesn't happen as we anticipated we are disappointed.

While some expectations are reasonable, many have no basis in reality whatsoever. If we expect to be loved (or at least liked) by everybody, we will be disappointed, as this is an unreasonable expectation. If we expect never to fail or make a mistake, we will also be in trouble. These may appear to be extreme examples, but subtle variations of these expectations are part of one's personality makeup. They center around spouse, children, parents, jobs, friends, and churches—and can be devastating in the disappointments they create.

We can deal effectively with our expectations by injecting a lot of "reality testing" into them. Ask yourself: "What law or principle says that such and such must happen? Would it not be better if I did not set myself up to expect something? Then, if it did happen, I could experience it as a surprise." I like to teach my clients the art of "bonus building." I say to them: "If you expect something to happen and it does not, you will be disappointed. If you do not expect it and it happens, you will have received a bonus." In other words, it is far better to receive bonuses (pleasures or surprises you did not expect) than disappointments.

The most important effect of this change in attitude is that the person affected does not experience all the unpleasant reactions that usually go along with disappointment. Emotions often disturb the social milieu and cause disturbances between spouses, children, church members, and so on. The wife who is disappointed because she is not kissed after her husband comes home from work may become angry and pout the rest of the evening. Her husband does not understand why she responds this way and eventually gets angry. Very soon an angry stalemate sets in. If the expectation by the wife was not set up in the first place, the emotional conflict could have been avoided and the social setting maintained in a more pleasant atmosphere. The real issue that gives rise to the expectation—the wife's need for her husband's affection—can then be discussed in a calm, anger-free environment. The issue stands a better chance of being resolved when there is a calm atmosphere than when anger and counteranger prevail.

ASSUMPTIONS are something we take for granted. In this context, they refer to the tendencies we have to take for granted what people say or do for us. A husband may make a dinner reservation and assume that his wife remembers that he told her he was going to do this two weeks before. When his wife acts surprised, he reacts with anger. Perhaps you assume that a friend will know where and at what time to pick you up for some engagement. If he fails to fulfill your assumptions, you react with anger. It seems that it is a very common human trait to make assumptions about many things that affect our relationships with others. These assumptions are mostly caused by faulty communication or just plain laziness in failing to check out the correctness of our information. As with so many other human weaknesses, we seldom take active steps to correct the behavior.

PERCEPTIONS: Early in our marriage my wife came home one day and said, "I saw the strangest thing today. I was coming out of the supermarket, and a motor car turned the corner in front of me, and it had only three wheels."

"You mean," I replied, "it was a three-wheeler?"

"No, it was a regular car, but it was riding on only three wheels."

Well, you can imagine how I responded to such a ludicrous idea. "Come on now—no ordinary car can stand just on three wheels.

Why do you think we use a jack to change a tire?"

And so I argued, but she was adamant: "The car only had three wheels, one wheel was missing."

Very soon it became a full-blown argument and for many months afterwards it was a source of disagreement between us. I thought, *Why could she not understand the laws of nature?* She probably thought, *Why does he not believe me when I tell him what I saw?* Well, what eventually resolved the matter for me was the realization that things are not always what they seem. "Seeing" is only perceiving, and "perception" is always subject to distortion. Unfortunately, the trouble is that we believe what we perceive. We believe what we think we see. What is actually true may be quite different. What my wife probably saw was only a perception. Due to the shadows cast by the car, its angle, and some other factors, she only perceived three of the car's four wheels. For her, though, the perception was reality, and I was failing to recognize the accuracy of her perception.

In the realm of our ideas and thoughts, we are also subject to the distortion of perception. It is absolutely essential that we realize three important facts about the way we perceive things, even psychologically:

1. It is not the facts of a situation that determine how we react but our *perception* of the situation.
2. The way we perceive something may be quite different from what actually happened.
3. We must always give others credit for the way they perceive things and not insist that it is only the *facts* that are important.

Arguments between friends and couples arise so often over differences in the way they perceive things that I am almost tempted to say that it is the most important single cause of interpersonal friction. Misperceptions cause confused communication and create issues where no issues exist.

If your wife says to you that she thinks you are too friendly with your best friend's wife, what is important is that she *perceives* it this way. If you insist, according to the facts, that she is wrong, become upset at the fact that she can even make such a suggestion, and demand that she retract such an accusation, you are making the fundamental mistake of not recognizing the importance of perceptions. You are failing to realize that what is important is *not* the fact that you have no ulterior motive, but that from her perspective what you are doing is causing her to perceive the situation as she does. Give her credit for her perception, and ask yourself whether you are to blame for the way she perceives the situation. This should open the way to better communication and move you to be more understanding and tolerant.

Which Come First—Feelings or Thoughts?

No doubt my emphasis on thoughts as the cause of feelings may lead some to ask, "Which comes first? Is it not possible that it is the feeling or emotion that *causes* the thought?" Yes, this is possible, but it appears to be much less frequently the case than the other way around. The best way to understand what happens is to realize that thoughts and feelings are a two-way street. If a thought occurs first and then creates a feeling, very soon this feeling influences the thought. If a feeling arises first, it generates a set of thoughts—and these thoughts then interact with the feeling. Much psychology has focused on and emphasized the *feelings-producing-thoughts* sequence, but in recent years this emphasis has begun to move to a greater appreciation of how thoughts produce feelings. Both approaches are important, and neither should be neglected. I have chosen to place greater emphasis on how thoughts work to influence feelings because of the relative neglect of this approach.

Thought processes are not only important in creating feelings but also serve to *maintain* feelings. Emotions receive their sustenance from the continuous things we say to ourselves. It appears to be extremely difficult to sustain an emotional upset without bolstering it by repeated ideas and thoughts. If someone insults you—and you become angry—you can only keep on being angry if you *continue* to say to yourself, "How could he [she] say such a horrible thing to me?" If you stop doing this and challenge the accuracy of how you interpret the insult, you can recover from the effects of the insult very much more quickly.

The Importance of Self-Talk

As I have indicated above, most of our thoughts take the form of conversations with ourselves. We could call this self-talk and are not always aware of doing this. As an exercise, you may wish to observe your thoughts more closely and identify the conversations you have with yourself. You might be quite surprised! When everything is pleasant and we are happy we say to ourselves, "This is good!" and when we experience unhappy things we say in effect, "This is bad!" We cannot have thoughts without this self-talk. Unfortunately, this self-talk is usually more illogical and irrational than when we converse with others. This is why we can often clear up our muddled thinking by talking something over with someone else. In the process of verbalizing our self-talk we see issues more clearly and can reduce our muddled thinking.

If you are going to learn how to reduce your disturbing emotional experiences, you will have to monitor very closely what you say to yourself. By so doing you can find clues to your irrational beliefs, attitudes, expectations, assumptions, and perceptions. In fact, self-talk can serve very effectively as a window onto your thoughts.

You can take the monitoring of your thoughts a step further and actively begin to interject healthier ideas into your thought stream. Instead of saying to yourself, "It makes me angry to hear her criticize my daughter," you could say, "It is most unfortunate that she finds it necessary to criticize my daughter. When she is over it, I'll have a quiet chat with her about it." Instead of self-talk that says, "It's terrible that I have to put up with such incompetence on the committee," you could say, "I'll have to make do with the best talent available. Perhaps we'll learn how to work together better."

These are just a few examples of how we can turn apparent and self-made catastrophes into positive experiences. Our natural tendency is to always look on the negative side—mainly, I suppose, because the only way we can feel good about ourselves is to criticize others. We find it hard to resist the need to catastrophize, and we exaggerate disaster out of all proportion and then spend our energy dwelling on the disaster rather than on the steps needed to remedy the situation. It takes deliberate action to turn these thoughts around and to say the right things to yourself.

Let me quote James Allen once again: "There is no physician like cheerful thought for dissipating ills; there is no comforter to compare with good will for dispersing the shadows of grief and sorrow. To live continually in thoughts of ill will, cynicism, suspicion, and envy, is to be confined in a self-made prison hole."

Summary

Do you want to be free? Do you want to be in control of your emotions and not have them control you and be so unafraid of them that they don't have to be avoided? Do you, as a Christian, want your emotions to enhance your spiritual life rather than work against it? You can only do this if you rise up and begin influencing your thoughts. The stream of your thoughts will be the most important factor which influences how you feel. If you can keep your hand firmly on the wheel of your thoughts, you will not be subjected to extremes of emotional buffeting. If you watch, control, and alter your thoughts by patient practice and trace their effects upon you and others, you can move yourself to the place of emotional freedom. I trust that the remainder of this book will help you do this, and that we will discover together that Solomon was right when he said, "For as a man thinketh in his heart, so is he . . ." (*see* Proverbs 23:7 KJV).

Additional Reading

1. *As a Man Thinketh*. James Allen. Old Tappan, New Jersey: Fleming H. Revell.
2. *Fully Human, Fully Alive*. John Powell. Niles, Illinois: Argus Communications.
3. *The Wider Place*. Eugenia Price. Grand Rapids, Michigan: Zondervan.
4. *You Can Become the Person You Want to Be*. Robert H. Schuller. Old Tappan, New Jersey: Fleming H. Revell.
5. *A New Guide to Rational Living*. Albert Ellis and Robert A. Harper. North Hollywood, California: Wilshire Books.
6. Philippians 2:1–16.

4

The Problem of Anger

CONTEMPORARY PSYCHOLOGY has not yet found an answer
to the problem of anger, although there is probably no other emotion that has caused as much confusion and disagreement among
psychologists. The subject has provoked so many different ideas
about how to deal with it that the average layperson must feel
utterly frustrated every time he reads a book by a psychologist.
Almost every self-help book has something to say about anger,
and there is little agreement amongst the writers about the "how
to." What all this means is that psychologists really do not understand the problem of anger. We may know a few things about it.
We know that it can elevate the blood pressure; that for some
reason we can actually enjoy being angry; that the capacity for
anger is built into our nervous systems; and that anger probably
serves some primitive, instinctual, protective purpose in helping
us overcome obstacles that block the way to our survival.

But is anger good for us? Are we better off if we allow ourselves
to be angry, or should we try to control our anger? Is anger stored
up, requiring some sort of release occasionally? Do we have to
show that we are angry, or is it sufficient to merely acknowledge
but hide it? Do we sin when we get angry? These and many
similar questions bombard our minds when we think about anger,
and psychology has not come to any agreement on what the

answers to these questions should be.

Theology does not seem to have helped us much either. I deal in therapy with many who claim to be Christians, including ministers, who have not come to terms with their anger. They experience much conflict over what to do with their anger and the consequent guilt which often creates a depression. Much sincere preaching condemns anger either directly or by inference, and Christian communities do not provide a clear understanding of the nature of anger or how to deal with it. While I do not want to give the impression that I have discovered the key to unlocking this puzzle, I do believe that there are a number of important principles that can help us in the dilemma. Perhaps exploring these with me can help you in your struggle against anger.

Anger and the Christian

Many well-meaning Christians find themselves caught in a struggle over their anger. On the one hand they get the message that anger is bad. They feel so "unchristian" whenever they give expression to their anger. Their communities discourage any show of anger, and this leads to a pervasive fear of making people angry and of dealing with someone who is angry. Because all angry feelings must be suppressed, group activities become difficult and often unpleasant experiences, and committee meetings mean pain and frustration. I can recall some of my own frustrating experiences in working with church committees where no expression of anger was tolerated. Every hint of bad feelings caused a chain of reactions which could not be handled by any of the parties concerned. Relationships became reduced to superficial encounters, and everyone kept everyone else at an emotional arm's length so as to avoid being hurt.

On the other hand, much contemporary psychology has emphasized that anger should be freely and uncontrollably expressed. We are encouraged to lash out at everything and everybody we please. "Don't bottle it up, but let your anger out!" we are encouraged on every hand. Our culture has almost come to worship those people who can be angry all the time. We admire them in some therapy groups and believe they are the only put-together and free people.

One current popular book on anger even suggests that every person should develop a variety of rituals for releasing bottled-up anger, and the impression I get in reading such advice is that life consists of a continuous struggle to find ways for blowing off anger-steam at every opportunity. I have a sneaking suspicion that the people who practice this are miserable within themselves as well as toward those with whom they live. Unfortunately, everyone else has to pay the price for the privilege that the angry person claims for himself.

Parents also often believe that children should be brought up being allowed to have temper tantrums as frequently as they like. They teach their children (if not directly, then certainly by their example) how to kick the furniture, the cat, and anything else that gets in their way, in order to ventilate their angry feelings. Unfortunately, the long-term effects of this behavior are not appreciated, especially since this can easily become a deeply entrenched life-style if it is encouraged. Such individuals usually end up acting this way all their lives, making things unpleasant for everyone else in their environment.

The Dilemma

There is something very satisfying about giving in to your anger. No doubt you have found this out for yourself. You have let go and lashed out at everything around you and have found this better than the utter frustration of having to bottle up your rage. But no sooner have you done this than you have been overcome by a deep sense of guilt and found yourself in the dilemma of not really knowing what you should do with your anger. Believing on the one hand that anger is condemned and should therefore be suppressed, yet deriving so much relief from ventilating anger, you are left feeling either extremely guilty for letting go or more frustrated and angry from having to bottle it up. But is anger condemned? Is there not a difference between the emotion of anger and its expression as hostility and aggression? We are told that it is healthier to express one's anger than to suppress it. The expression of anger is indeed a healthier alternative than suppressing it. But is there not an even healthier way—that of not having anger at all? Is there a constructive and creative way to deal with angry feelings without compromising one's faith and causing discomfort to others? I believe there is. A proper understanding of anger and its mysterious workings is essential to the building of community, whether this community has to do with intimate relationships such as marriage and the family, or with larger community life as in the church. Effective committee work requires a clear understanding of the dynamics of anger, and maturity in the Christian faith can only be achieved as one makes progress in mastering one's anger.

The Nature of Anger

We all know what anger feels like—but do we know what it is? One unabridged dictionary defines it as "a strong feeling of displeasure excited by a real or supposed injury: often accompanied by a desire to take vengeance or to obtain satisfaction from the offending party." The key words in this definition are *strong feeling, injury,* and *vengeance.* Anger always has these three components, and we will see that the key to dealing with anger lies in dealing with these components.

While anger may have served some function for human beings in more primitive settings and may now be useful in emergency situations, the everyday life we all live seldom calls for legitimate anger. It is nearly always destructive in relationships and is often hazardous to our health. The prolonged experience of anger has been linked by some theorists to problems such as high blood pressure (essential hypertension). Anger disturbs our happiness and seldom moves us toward being fulfilled persons. It disturbs marriages and often incapacitates and immobilizes us. Severe anger can even be a form of temporary insanity, since this implies that the person is completely out of control and dangerous to those around. Most child- and wife-beatings take place under conditions of extreme anger, and even murder is committed when the need to take vengeance is overwhelming.

Is Anger Ever Necessary?

Under what conditions is anger essential and necessary? Do we ever have to get angry—or could we get by without it? In our modern life-style the real need for anger as an essential emotion seldom arises. Occasions where we need anger for our survival must surely be very rare. I can think of one such occasion that occurred recently with a colleague of mine, and this will serve to illustrate my point that anger as an essential emotion is seldom legitimately needed. Waiting for his daughter one evening, my colleague was sitting with his wife and a friend in his automobile outside an apartment building. Three young men with revolvers accosted them and asked that they hand over their money and jewelry. My colleague, a senior professor in his early eighties, was sitting in the backseat. He was utterly stunned while these men began removing the jewelry from the two women in the front, one of the men holding the revolver at his wife's head. At first the robbers did not notice him in the back of the car, but finally one of the men saw him and came around to open his door. As the car door began to open, my colleague became extremely angry at the outrage and—overcoming all fear and disregarding the consequences for himself—he kicked out with both his feet. The young man went flying, and his friends panicked and fled. Discussing the incident afterwards, my colleague felt that it was anger that gave him the courage to do what he did. Anger has the ability to trigger resources and enables us to perform tasks we could not otherwise do. It motivates us to overcome obstacles, and the display of anger can protect us by frightening away assailants. In more primitive cultures and in the animal world, we see clear evidence for this use of anger. In our modern life-style and western culture, however, we seldom need to make use of anger legitimately. Life is far more "psychological" and less "physical" for most of us, our obstacles more subtle, our enemies less tangible, and our fears mostly imagined. Of what value, then, is anger under such conditions? Perhaps it is because we no longer have a legitimate outlet for anger that it has become a major problem for us and a serious disturbing factor in our relationships.

A Model for Understanding Anger

Our culture does not teach us how to handle anger; rather we are trained to suppress it or give expression to it in devious ways.

In order to be able to cope with anger, it is useful to have a clear understanding of how anger arises.While the model of anger I will present here is somewhat simplistic, it contains the essential elements for understanding the problem and can be used with confidence to guide you in coming to understand the nature of anger as you experience it.

Figure 1 presents this model. There are four levels to be considered: the origins of anger, its causes, its expressions, and its resolution.

The origins of anger. For the origins of anger we need to consider both the biological and the learned components, as both contribute to the creation of anger within us. Anger is one of the primary emotions present at birth. If you hold a baby down so that he cannot move, you will elicit the instinctive rage response which is necessary for survival. Specific parts of the brain have been identified as being responsible for the anger response. Whenever a particular provoking stimulus is experienced, the neural system responsible for anger becomes activated. It is possible to activate parts of the brain directly through electrical stimulation and thus elicit an anger response. The important point for us, however, is that the normal stimulus that activates the anger response is purely psychological. In other words, the ideas, thoughts, and perceptions we experience and our interpretation of these events trigger our anger response, and these triggers are acquired primarily through learning. There is, therefore, an important connection between what we are thinking and experiencing and the inbuilt, biologically determined mechanism of anger. It takes a thought to trigger anger. The implication of this will become clear as we proceed.

The causes of anger. Anger can be caused or triggered through four main mechanisms: *frustration, hurt, conditioned response,* and *instinctive protection.* The first two are probably more important from our point of view, since they are most likely to be the major cause of anger for us, given our westernized lifestyle.

FRUSTRATION: One of the more important theories about anger that has been developed is called the "frustration-hostility-aggression" theory. It states that anger is the consequence of

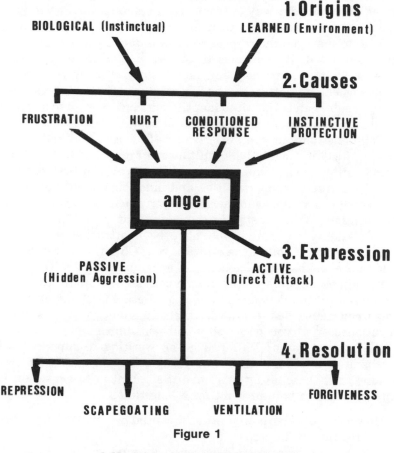

Figure 1

A Model for Understanding Anger

frustration or thwarting. When you desire something strongly and cannot get it, you become angry because your need is frustrated. Primitively, this anger is intended to help you overcome the obstacle by provoking you to overcome or attack it.

Obstacles can take many forms, and anything that prevents you from obtaining any of your desired goals has the potential for creating anger. Obstacles can be *physical:* breaking a leg the day before you are due to play an important game, or having the car break down on your way to work. They can be *social:* when your spouse won't agree to go to a movie with you, when someone refuses to show you the respect you feel is due to you, or when you are humiliated. We can also have *personal* obstacles: low self-esteem, feelings of inadequacy, or a history of being rejected by others as being unattractive or incompetent. These obstacles can be very subtle and difficult to identify but can give rise to as much frustration and anger as any physical obstacle.

Conflict situations can also give rise to frustration and anger. By "conflict" is meant the simultaneous arousal of two or more incompatible goals. This occurs when we are torn between two equally attractive opportunities and must choose only one. Are you going to give up a summer fishing trip to be with your family on vacation? Will you stay in a marriage situation for the children's sake, even though you have been attracted to another partner? Will you follow the ethics of your Christian commitment and thus avoid having a "good time" on a business trip? These are illustrations of some of the major conflict situations that can arise. Not all conflicts are as major as these, but even petty conflicts can cause just as much frustration and anger as those mentioned. Will you go to play golf—or support your son at a Little League game? Will you go on working to support your husband in graduate school—or will you get on with your own studies? All these situations have the potential to cause anger and keep it at a boiling point for a long time.

How do we deal with anger that is caused by frustration? There are three important steps:

1. *Develop a more flexible personality*. Improve your ability to adapt to changing situations. Rigidity in your expectations and responses is a sure sign of neurotic tendencies. You can do this in a number of ways. For instance, keep a careful lookout for events in your life that cause you to become angry, no matter how small they may appear to be. As soon as you realize you are angry, try to

see whether you can identify the presence of frustration. Is there something you want that you can't get? Is someone blocking your way? Have you lost something or are you about to lose something? Frustration can take many forms, and it may be necessary for you to discuss the matter with a family member or close friend in order to identify it. Pay attention to how you feel and especially to what you are saying to yourself. Remind yourself that you need to be flexible, and let go of anything you may be clinging to unnecessarily. Doing this deliberately and consciously gives you the feeling of being in control and maximizes your ability to be flexible.

You can better prepare your children for handling frustration in their lives by teaching them that they don't need to receive everything they want immediately. Low frustration tolerance in children (and later in adult life) is a common symptom of our age and is the cause of much unhappiness. We perpetuate this low tolerance for frustration in our children when we give them everything they want *immediately.* Learning how to delay gratification and postpone the fulfillment of our desires is an important step towards maturity and a healthy emotional life. We cannot always get everything we want immediately! Irrationally, though, we set ourselves up to expect just this and consequently experience repeated frustration and anger.

2. *Learn to accept and be happy with compromises.* In the minds of some, the word *compromise* is not acceptable. It implies that you lower your standards, your ideals, and your goals—and settle for something that is second class. I don't mean this, but I do believe that most of us are hung up on "perfection." We are obsessed with wanting to be perfect mothers, fathers, children, lovers, workers, and students. We abhor failure and try to avoid it at every opportunity. We despise ourselves every time we fail or show any signs of imperfection. We have great difficulty accepting our humanness, our incompleteness. We are *not* gods! Christ came to save imperfect people (which we *all* are), and while we remain imperfect we will have to accept the reality of our human limitations.

3. *Work at knowing yourself.* What motivates you? What

causes you to react the way you do? I never cease to marvel at how naive we are about ourselves. We know a lot about how our friends function and don't hesitate to give advice when necessary. We know little about ourselves, and nowhere is this ignorance more damaging than in the area of frustration and anger. If we do not know *when* we are frustrated or *what* frustrates us, we will not be able to deal with our anger. Frustrated dependency needs, ego needs, love needs, security needs, and a host of other needs can keep us constantly experiencing periods of anger over which we have no control—simply because we don't understand ourselves.

HURT: The next important cause of anger is *hurt*. Such anger can arise whenever we experience physical or psychological pain. Have you ever had someone tramp on your toe? The pain you experience triggers a reaction of anger and a strong desire to hurt back. Children demonstrate this to us again and again. Johnny pulls Mary's hair, and immediately Mary wants to do the same thing back to Johnny. When we grow up we merely substitute humiliating or other psychological pain for the hair pulling. Psychological pain can produce just as strong a desire to hurt back. If you are criticized, do you stand there calmly and take it? Not if you are human. Even if you do not give expression to your feelings, in the back of your mind you are tearing the other person apart with countercriticism and faultfinding. Most sarcasm is merely a subtle way of hurting back. I will return to this form of anger and discuss its solution in the next chapter.

CONDITIONED RESPONSES: These causes for anger are learned early in life. We learn how to get our way by displaying anger. Parents, teachers, brothers, and sisters reinforce this behavior by giving us our own way. We can remove obstacles and manipulate our friends by shows of anger. Sometimes we show the anger in more subtle ways, such as pouting, negativity, and threatening. The temper tantrum of a child is a good example of a conditioned anger response. On the very first occasion of such a tantrum, the child may only have experienced a frustrating response to not getting what he wanted. The anger outburst which followed was embarrassing to the parent, who then gave in to the wishes of the child. If this is repeated a few times, the child quickly learns (quite unconsciously) that when he becomes angry and causes a disturbance he can get everything he desires—and the temper-tantrum pattern has become established. The temper-tantrum anger is, of course, more intense than the original frustration-anger, and the child gives it a flare and lots of noise to accentuate its manipulative purpose. These children learn how to substitute other forms of anger when they grow up, but basically they continue to utilize conditioned forms of anger in order to manipulate people and get their way. I call this "emotional blackmailing," and it is very common in dysfunctional people.

INSTINCTIVE PROTECTION: I have already drawn attention to the fact that anger can serve as a form of instinctive protection. It provides us with the motivating force and courage we use to overcome obstacles and defend ourselves. In this sense it is a healthy form of anger. However, our present life-style, which does not call for physical means of self-protection in ordinary life encounters, seldom demands that we use this form of anger. The major causes for our problems with anger lie clearly in the areas of frustration, hurt, and conditioned response.

The resolution of anger.   We resort to a number of devices for resolving the anger we experience. Not all of these ways are helpful or healthy. The three most common are *repression, scapegoating,* and *ventilation.* I believe that *forgiveness* is the New Testament's answer to the problem of anger and will discuss this in more detail in the next chapter.

REPRESSION of anger has always been known to be harmful. Holding back your anger, forcing it out of your awareness, and denying that it even exists can cause you many problems. You run the risk of developing such psychosomatic disorders as high blood pressure, tension headache, muscular fatigue, and gastric disturbances. It is psychologically damaging because it disturbs your relationships with others and prevents you from getting at the real issues between yourself and other people. Holding back your anger does not eliminate it but causes it rather to find other ways to be expressed. This can distort your perspective on important life issues and cause you to become cynical and a misery to be around. Of course, I am not advocating that one should give unrestrained expression to all one's anger. But there is a big difference between expressing one's anger in a destructive way and using it creatively and constructively.

SCAPEGOATING refers to the tendency to take the anger that belongs in one place and dump it on another. The real cause for the anger never receives the anger reaction. A much "safer" person or object is usually the one to receive it. When you have been bawled out by your employer for some mistake you have made and cannot express anger toward him, you may go home and immediately find something to criticize or get angry at in your home. "Watch out, Mom, kids, cats and dogs! Here comes Dad and he is mad again!" is so common an attitude in the many families I have worked with that I have become convinced that it is as American as apple pie! Scapegoating is so common in all of our relationships that we hardly even recognize when it is taking place. I suppose it is only human nature to want to take out our anger on a safer person or object, but doing this day in and day out must eventually have a detrimental effect on our relatives and friends (not to mention our pets).

The origin of the term *scapegoating* is interesting and helps us understand its nature. It comes from the Old Testament reference to the innocent goat which was brought to the altar by the High Priest (*see* Leviticus 16:20–22). Laying both hands on the goat's head, the High Priest confessed all the sins of the people. The goat was then taken out into the wilderness and allowed to go free, thus symbolically taking all the sins of the people into a land that was uninhabited. Don't you feel like this goat at times? Innocent. You have done nothing wrong. Suddenly you become the recipient of a lot of anger, heaped on your head by your wife or husband, your adolescent child, a parent, or a friend. You know you didn't cause the anger. Why should they get angry with you? Why can't they direct their anger back at its real source? Worst of all, they won't even acknowledge that they are really angry at someone else, and you don't even have the relief of finding a new uninhabited country you can run to for yourself. This is the trap many find themselves in, and more misery and disturbed relationships are caused by inappropriate scapegoating of anger than any other emotional factor. If you are guilty of this, take heart; it's not that difficult to change. I know—because I've been able to! Part of the problem is solved just by admitting that this is what you do. The rest comes from careful attention to the ideas I will present in the next chapter.

VENTILATION is the term used by many contemporary psychologists (fortunately not all of them) to describe the best method for the resolution of anger. Those who advocate this position take the view that it is desirable and even a dire necessity that we let out all our angry feelings and hostility at all times. They insist that it is bad for us to bottle up our anger and that good only comes from attacking—with words, foam-rubber bats, and tennis rackets—everything and everybody causing us anger. Some parents who have accepted this point of view allow their children to cut up and destroy their toys, throw stones at other objects, and even encourage their children to go into their rooms and scream their heads off, believing that the discharge of pent-up anger is beneficial and that the urge to destroy is normal and necessary and must even be encouraged.

My instinct and my understanding of the Gospel's message tells me that there is something wrong with this approach or even a watered-down version. I have worked in therapy with enough angry people to know that while helping them to get angry more frequently and encouraging them to express it more openly may be emotionally satisfying, it neither removes the cause for the anger nor drains away the angry feelings at all times. Above all else, this approach does not help people to come to terms with their frustration proneness nor teach them how to heal their hurts. There is enough experimental psychological evidence to show that such "ventilation" techniques for dealing with anger—where one allows the anger to express itself in violent words and actions—only serve to reduce controls against anger and encourage more frequent use of aggressive behavior in order to vent anger feelings. There is tremendous secondary benefit to be derived from expressing anger, but this does not cure the anger problem. One study showed that children who were originally low in aggressive behavior and who were given free-play experiences with aggressive toys became significantly more aggressive in their behavior after playing with these toys, presumably because the aggressive make-believe activity lowered their normal restraints against aggression. Playing with aggressive toys does not drain away anger. Rather, it opens up new ways for expressing anger and for translating anger into hostility. Aggressive behavior is, in many respects, self-rewarding and inherently satisfying, so that it can easily become entrenched as a behavior style without serving any anger-release advantages.

Ventilation techniques for resolving anger appear to be effective because of one simple mechanism: translating anger into aggression and hostility. I think it is very important to make a distinction between *anger* (the feeling component) and *aggression and hostility* (the behavior which expresses the anger). By transforming anger (the feeling) into hostility (the behavior arising from the anger), we can provide a way for resolving the anger. It has been shown experimentally that when anger is provoked, blood pressure becomes elevated. If the object causing the anger is attacked, the blood pressure rapidly decreases. If no attack is allowed and the person is left alone, it takes a little while for the pressure to return to normal. The translation of the anger feeling into an action of attack provides relief from the feeling as well as from the consequent physiological reaction. It is this mechanism which is utilized when one encourages someone to ventilate his anger and express it in action.

But is this the only way to resolve angry feelings? Does this not ignore the long-term effects of these expressive actions? Would this behavior not create further conflicting situations in the environment of those around, such that further anger is generated by their reactions? I once had a woman come to me after a lecture I had given on "The Christian and Anger" and tell me about her best friend's eighteen-year-old daughter who had been in therapy for two years. The teenager was somewhat withdrawn and passive in her personality when she first started psychotherapy, but shortly after she commenced, she became very hostile and angry.

It was at the insistence of her therapist that she began lashing out angrily at everyone around her. She found this behavior so rewarding that after two years it had become an established personality style with her. Unfortunately, neither her mother, her mother's friend who related the story to me, nor anyone else in the girl's life found this to be pleasant, and she soon became ostracized by her friends. The question that this woman posed to me was: "Is she better off after such therapy than she would have been if left as she was?" I could not say with any certainty whether she would have been better without the therapy, but I do know that there is a better way to deal with anger than to translate it into hostility and aggression.

This is not to say that there are no therapeutic benefits to be derived from the use of ventilation techniques. These techniques, used carefully and under the supervision of an experienced therapist, can speed up therapy and bring much needed relief to those who cannot cope with their anger. However, they should only be used by trained professionals, as there is a high probability that the person so helped will act aggressively outside of the therapy situation as well. What is, therefore, a very effective therapeutic technique should be contained within the therapy situation and should not be allowed to become a norm for everyday living. A legitimate therapeutic technique is not necessarily a legitimate life-style.

Anger and the Gospel

The need to differentiate between *anger* (the feeling) and *hostility/aggression* (the behavior arising out of the feeling) is even more important when we turn to understanding the New Testament's approach to the problem of anger. The Apostle Paul presents us with what at first seems to be an impossible paradox: "Be ye angry, and sin not: let not the sun go down upon your wrath" (Ephesians 4:26 KJV).

How can one be angry and sin not? The New English Bible translation makes a little clearer what the Apostle Paul was saying and provides us with a very up-to-date understanding not only of the nature of anger but also of its solution: "If you are

angry, do not let anger lead you into sin; do not let sunset find
you still nursing it . . . ."

My understanding of what Paul is saying here is that it is not
the anger itself (as feeling) that is wrong, but that anger has the
potential for leading you into sin. The point is that it is the translation or conversion of anger feelings into aggressive and hostile
acts that leads us into sin. To feel anger, to tell someone that you
feel angry, and to talk about your anger are both healthy and
necessary. As long as you recognize the anger as your own and
avoid hurting back the object of your anger, you are keeping it as
a feeling—and all feelings are legitimate! What you *do* with your
feeling may not be, and this is where you can fall into sin!

The context of Paul's injunction makes his intention very clear.
Both here in Ephesians 4, as well as in Romans 12 (where he
deals with the revengeful aspects of anger), the control of anger is
placed in the context of the need for unity in "the body of Christ."
In the immediately preceding verse, he tells us; "Then throw off
falsehood; speak the truth to each other, for all of us are the parts
of one body" (Ephesians 4:25 NEB). The need for harmony within
the body dictates that anger must somehow be controlled or
channeled into nondestructive outlets. Whether the "body" is the
church, as Paul intends here, or the home or the office, harmonious relationships are only possible where there is a healthy anger
atmosphere. Nothing is more destructive to relationships than
anger that has been uncontrollably transformed into hostile and
aggressive acts.

The reasons why anger has so much potential for leading us
into sin are not difficult to identify:

1. Our lower nature wants revenge. I will deal with this
more fully in the next chapter, but let me point out here that
anger which is the result of hurt is often, if not always, accompanied by a strong desire to take vengeance or obtain satisfaction
from the one who has hurt us. This response tendency is built into
us. That is why Paul has to admonish us: "Never pay back evil for
evil . . . . If possible, so far as it lies with you, live at peace with
all men. My dear friends, *do not seek revenge* . . . ." (Romans
12:17–19 NEB; italics added).

While we would probably never openly acknowledge these deep tendencies, our attitude toward those who hurt us betrays us every time.

2. The emotion of anger is a very powerful controller of our behavior. Anger has potential for sin because we lose control of ourselves. We can then no longer be responsible for what we do. Anger takes over like a gale-force wind and determines the direction we go. Our tiny self-control rudder has little effect when the raging force of anger has taken over. Men have been known to murder under such conditions, and we are very naive if we do not recognize the power of anger to take over control of what we do and say.

3. Anger blocks our ability to love. Above all else, we are commanded to love one another. We cannot do this when we are giving expression to anger. Anger will motivate us to hate, wound, damage, despise, curse, scold, and humiliate. We cannot love under these conditions, and everything we stand for is in danger of being destroyed when we allow anger to be transformed into any of these hostile words and actions.

An emotion with the potential for so much sin needs to be avoided as much as possible. Anger (as feeling) may be inevitable in our lives, and we certainly must accept it as a normal response whenever it occurs. So as to reduce its potential for sin, it would be far better, however, if we could learn how not to trigger the anger in the first place, and—if it is already triggered—how to resolve it quickly. (Paul's time limit is before the sun sets.) How to resolve your anger effectively in a healthy way is the topic of the next chapter.

Summary

Even among psychologists, there is much confusion about the nature of anger and how best to deal with these feelings. There is a constructive way to deal with angry feelings without causing discomfort to others and—for the Christian—without compromising one's faith.

Greater understanding of the mechanisms of anger can be at-
tained through examining the origins of anger (biological and
learned); its causes (frustration, hurt, conditioned response, instinctive protection); passive and direct methods of expression;
and its resolution. The latter is represented most commonly by
repression, scapegoating, and *ventilation.*

Although each of these mechanisms may provide some relief
from the pressures of angry feelings, there are New Testament
answers which can lead to effective and healthy handling of this
powerful emotion.

Additional Reading

1. *The Angry Book.* Theodore I. Rubin. New York: Macmillan.
2. *How to Get Angry Without Feeling Guilty.* Adelaide Bry.
   New York: New American Library.
3. *Anger.* Leo Madow. New York: Scribner's.
4. Ephesians 4.

5

Freedom From Anger

IN THE PRECEDING CHAPTER I stated that while there are many ways we can deal with our anger, the concept of *forgiveness* holds out the most promise for aiding us in effectively resolving anger feelings once they have arisen. This concept is so important that I want to devote this chapter to showing how effective it can be and how central it is, especially to a Christian understanding of how to deal with anger. Forgiveness is at the heart of the Christian Gospel. It is the genius of Christianity, and not without reason. God knows who and what we are and He has both given and demonstrated forgiveness in a remarkable way. He knows that we need forgiveness, both for receiving it ourselves, as well as for us to give to others. As a psychologist, I am convinced that to know both how to receive and give forgiveness is crucial to the problem of anger.

The Frustration of Unresolved Anger

There will be many situations in which we will not be able to deal with our anger in any active way. Even if we could discuss our feelings with those who are causing the anger, we will not always have the satisfaction of an apology or even a clear understanding of our feelings—and we will frequently be left angrier than when we started out with the hope of working through our feelings with those concerned. Often the person causing the anger is inaccessible to us. It may be an employer, or the person may have died. How do we get satisfaction and resolve our anger in such cases? As I have already pointed out, transforming one's anger into hostility or aggression may help if it is done under controlled therapeutic conditions, but only a few have this opportunity available to them. I will try to show that when we are trapped in such an impasse we have only one course of action open to us. This course has been clearly charted for us in the New Testament writings and can be summed up in the concept of "forgiveness." I urge you to come to terms with it. Find out for yourself how freeing it can be for you to experience it and to know how to give it.

Don't think for one moment that this is easy. You need to understand forgiveness in the context of a number of other important concepts and needs, and these must all be woven into the fabric of your whole personality if you are going to be able to resolve your anger quickly.

Cut Off Your Anger at the Earliest Possible Moment

Before we look at the steps involved in resolving anger, let me stress how important it is for you to try to cut off your anger at the earliest possible moment, preferably at the trigger point. I find again and again in therapy with my clients that they don't realize that they have tremendous ability to avoid getting angry in the first place. Just recently a client told me that for many years her husband was able to make her become extremely angry—always over the same incident. It would be breaking a confidence to reveal specific details, but it was always the same incident that caused the anger response. Since it occurred with such regularity (and there was nothing she could do to change her husband's behavior), I asked my client why she continued to give this incident the power to make her angry. I reminded her that she was responsible for doing this and that she could stop this if she wanted to—merely by changing her attitude toward it. It was her husband's problem, and she did not have to let it make her angry. She changed her attitude and reduced the frequency of her anger reactions. This then paved the way to improved communication with her husband, and the marital relationship showed a dramatic turn for the better.

This client's story is by no means unusual or rare. We get angry without thinking about whether or not we could have avoided it. All anger has a point at which it begins (the trigger point), and there are a number of ways we can deal with our thoughts and attitudes, either to avoid the triggering or to cut off the anger at the earliest possible moment. Let us explore some of these before we go any further.

You can deal with your anger at four different points:

1. When you are calm and not bothered by any anger
2. Just before you respond in anger to some event
3. Just after you have become angry, but before you have transformed the anger into hostility
4. When your anger has become hostility

1. Dealing with anger in your sane moments. When you are calm and not experiencing any anger, you are in the best possible place for preparing yourself so as not to create anger unnecessarily. Examine your recent anger episodes and honestly face up to whether you could have avoided them altogether. Do you make unrealistic demands of others? Are you impatient and do you always want your own way? Do you set up unrealistic expectations or expect people to guess what you are thinking or wanting—and then get angry when they make a mistake?

If you have a low tolerance for frustration, you should work at raising this tolerance. You need to remind yourself that you cannot always get your own way. Others also have rights. People are only human. Motor mechanics *do* make mistakes and foul up repairs. Children *are* inconsiderate and inconsistent and won't necessarily change as they get older. Husbands do forget birthdays, and friends are *not always* considerate of your feelings. So why not build into your beliefs and expectations some allowance for human inadequacies, learn to tolerate these imperfections, and thus prevent getting angry and upset in the first place? If you do this, you will find that much of your anger is unnecessary and can be completely avoided with just a little bit of forethought and change in attitude. Use your prayer time, meditation, or devotions to upgrade your tolerance for frustration with the imperfection of others. Chart your anger responses carefully and see whether you are getting angry over the same thing again and again. If so, what is the reason? Talk to the person who constantly thwarts you or puts you down. Explain to him how you react to his behavior and explore with him ways for preventing it from happening again. In sum, try to remove the causes of your anger when you are calm and objective and have all your resources at your disposal.

2. Cutting off anger just before it begins.   Even though you may have done your homework well during your sane moments, there will be times when anger will tend to break through. Since life is full of frustrations and hurts, occasions for anger must inevitably arise. Careful preparation of your attitudes, as I have outlined in the previous section, can help you here also. Frequently you can see an anger episode coming. The signs of its raising its ugly head are difficult to miss. "There he goes again with his criticism." "She's going to nag me when I get home." "I wonder why he said that to me!" These are the typical self-conversations we have just before we get angry. With a little thought you could prepare a list of those self-talk statements that apply to yourself. As soon as you begin talking to yourself this way, you should stop and ask yourself, "Do I need to get angry? Will it help me handle the issue better?" At this point you *do* have a choice. You can proceed to develop the anger by your self-talk or you can decide to deal with the problem some other way. Merely believing that you have a choice can give you the freedom not to get angry.

3. When you are angry.   Assuming that you cannot avoid the trigger, what do you do with a fully developed anger feeling? First, *recognize your anger*. It sounds so simple, doesn't it? Do you know how hard it is to acknowledge your anger when you are angry? The anger tends to block out any awareness of itself, almost as if it were "afraid" that, once recognized, it would have to go away. We have a marked tendency to want to deny the presence of anger in ourselves. We see it as a sign of weakness and being out of control (which it is)—and we don't want anyone, including ourselves, to draw attention to it. Anger may be denied simply because we don't have a "legitimate" reason for being angry.

If you are not aware of your anger, it stands to reason that you cannot proceed with resolving it. If you resist acknowledging it, you will only aggravate the problem. To be angry and yet not willing to own up to that anger makes you a very difficult person to be around. If you are like this, is it any wonder that others find it difficult to love you?

How can you improve your anger recognition? Pray for sensitivity and self-honesty. Contract with a friend, your spouse, or a parent to tell you every time he or she perceives you as being angry. Do not be concerned about whether the perception is right or wrong. Your defense system may not allow you to admit to the anger. Ignore your own self-perception and take the other's at face value, and you will soon begin opening yourself up to greater self-honesty. This honesty only comes when you stop being defensive, and you can only teach yourself to stop being defensive when you accept as valid the perception that others have of you. If you are truly not angry when they say you are, you are none the worse, since following through on the remaining steps will be a good exercise for your soul. You are better off assuming that you are angry when others tell you that you are than continuing to stand your ground and increasing your defensiveness.

Second, *release vindictiveness*. Once you have admitted and owned up to your anger, the next step is to deal with the strong, almost inbuilt desire that you will have to hurt back and obtain satisfaction from the offending party. I must stress that this need to hurt back is present *every time* we are angered by being hurt. It can take such a subtle form that we may not recognize it, and our need to deny its presence may even be stronger than our need not to admit that we are angry. But it *is* there and must be dealt with before we can lay aside our anger.

It is a law of our lower nature that we want to hurt back when we are hurt. This probably serves some protective function to our beings, and in more primitive settings makes survival possible by motivating the one who is hurt to fight back. It becomes a much more subtle exercise in our modern life-style and doesn't always involve physical retaliation. We can see this law at work in the development of children. When they are very young, they will fight back every time they are hurt. At first it is merely a physical defense, but later on it becomes a desire to hurt back in order to even the score. Much later in life, of course, we learn how to psychologize the hurting back and substitute words for actions and psychological pain for physical pain.

The portion of the Sermon on the Mount in Matthew 5:38–48 is most illuminating on this point and provides us with some important principles for dealing with anger. Read this portion of Scripture in your favorite translation. Jesus is discussing our relationship to our enemies. Who are our enemies? Anyone who has the potential to hurt us! It can be a husband, a parent, a friend. Don't think of your enemy as being only someone on the other side of the world. Rather, it can be someone right in your own backyard and very close to you. How do you deal with your enemy—that person who has hurt you? You can easily misunderstand the point of what Jesus is saying if you focus too much on your enemy "getting away with it." We are so often afraid that the one who has hurt us will not get punished for his acts. "If I let him get away with that, he won't respect me and will do it to me over and over again!" is a common reaction to being hurt by someone, whether it is physical or psychological hurt. This reaction, of course, highlights the fact that we are often totally preoccupied with "balancing the score" whenever we are hurt. Just yesterday I received a citation for speeding. I was angry, even though I was guilty. I directed my anger at the officer and found my self-talk saying, "How can I get back at him?" Ridiculous, of course, but this is how we function.

What Jesus is doing here is simply telling us what we are like. The old law said we could take "an eye for an eye and a tooth for a tooth," and this law followed our basic instincts and let us do what we deep down wanted to do. But God knows that this natural tendency to want revenge and hurt back is so strong and overpowering that we do not know when to stop. Can we stop at just one eye? I doubt it. When will we have punished enough to even the score? History has taught us that when Jesus tells us to "turn the other cheek" or "go the extra mile," He is *not* telling us to give our enemy some advantage over us. He is doing this *for our pro-tection*. He is in effect saying, "Because you do not know what justice is, I cannot trust you with punishment. When someone hurts you, you are better off letting him hurt you again than trying to hurt him back." Our complex legal and penal system attests to these facts. "Cheek turning," therefore, is not for our enemy's advantage, but for our own protection. If we do not follow this principle, when we have finished punishing our enemy he will only be ready for his turn to punish us again—and the cycle will repeat itself over and over again. When such a cycle gets out of hand we call it "war."

This principle is important even when we discipline our children. Every act of discipline can be seen as comprising one part that has to do with a need to correct the behavior and another part that is a need to punish or hurt back, usually because of the pain that the misbehavior has caused.

When the need to punish is greater than the need to hurt back, we have the situation that is depicted in Figure 2.

Figure 2

Discipline With Too Much Punishment

If we lose our tempers when we discipline and punish excessively, we may not be correcting the faulty behavior at all. We
may set up so much anger and hostility as a reaction in the child
that his need to hurt us back prevents him from experiencing any
effective learning. This problem has led to much confusion on the
part of parents and a tendency in some contemporary psychology
to advise parents to withdraw completely and not discipline at all.
By careful design of our discipline procedures, however, we
should be able to reduce the contribution of our need to punish or
hurt back the child for the pain he has caused us. We can thus
maximize the component of discipline that is designed to correct the behavior. This situation would then be as shown in
Figure 3.

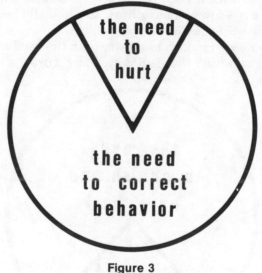

Figure 3
The Correct Way to Discipline

How do we do this? By doing exactly what we would do to
anyone hurting us, whether the anger is caused by our so-called
enemies or by our children. We must first free ourselves of any
vindictiveness and desire to hurt back. This is the essence of what
Jesus is saying in Matthew 5. Cheek turning does not mean that

we become doormats and let everyone trample over us. If we allowed this, we would be having a problem with assertiveness, in that we are unable to stand up for our rights. Cheek turning is not intended to be the act of a coward, nor is it meant to perpetuate an attitude of domination by one person over another. Neither is it intended to be the "behavior of confusion," in which one does not have the ability to stand up for or be oneself. It is simply a recognition of who we are and that when we are hurt we have a very strong urge to hurt back. God asks us to leave all punishment to Him. There is ample evidence in the history of humankind (as well as in your own history, I am sure) that when we hurt back we do not know when to stop. The Old Testament's principle of "an eye for an eye and a tooth for a tooth" is difficult to put into practice when you are the one who is hurting. We want an eye, a tooth, and a foot for every eye we lose. We just do not know when the scales are balanced and when or how to stop. God has therefore laid down this important principle for us, which Paul reemphasizes in Romans:

> Never pay back evil for evil. Let your aims be such as all men count honourable. If possible, so far as it lies with you, live at peace with all men. My dear friends, do not seek revenge, but leave a place for divine retribution . . . .
>
> Romans 12:17–19 NEB

But how do we give up this need to hurt back? Paul is very clear in Ephesians 4 on how this can be done. After reminding us in verse 26 about anger's potential for leading us into sin, he proceeds to say: "Have done with spite and passion, all angry shouting and cursing, and bad feeling of every kind. Be generous to one another, tender-hearted, *forgiving* one another as God in Christ forgave you" (vv. 31, 32 NEB; italics added).

Forgiveness is the key to giving up your need to hurt back, and the genius of Christianity is in the fact that forgiveness of others is made possible through God's forgiveness of us.

What is forgiveness? This I am often asked by well-meaning Christians. In the context of the Scripture portions I have already cited, I would define *forgiveness* as follows: FORGIVENESS IS SURRENDERING MY RIGHT TO HURT YOU BACK IF YOU HURT ME.

Print this in large letters and stick it on your bedroom mirror to remind you of it each day. I can confidently say that you will not be able to resolve the anger in your life until you have learned how to put this in practice. I would even go further and say that under no circumstances should you approach anyone about your anger with a view to "talking it out" until you have first taken the step of surrendering your right to hurt back. Your need for revenge will be too strong and can take so many subtle forms that you will only humiliate and embarrass the one who has hurt you. I know of many who will go so far as to fantasize killing or maiming the other person. Even asking someone to apologize can be seen as a "hurt back" maneuver. By insisting that others apologize, we cause them the pain of humiliation. This is, in fact, how hurting back operates to resolve our anger. As soon as we perceive the other person as having experienced enough pain to balance our pain, we may give up our anger. Unfortunately, in obtaining our satisfaction we have left the other person hurting and created in him a need to retaliate. The cycle repeats itself over and over again until, if we are fortunate, it gradually dies out. Forgiving cuts right across all of this—which is what it is designed to do!

From past experience, I know what you may be thinking right now: "Yes, that sounds so easy, but putting it into practice is another matter." It *is* difficult, but this doesn't mean it isn't the right way. I know of no better motivating force than the remembrance of God's forgiveness through Christ. Remind yourself that forgiving others is not just optional but mandatory. Your forgiveness from God is dependent upon your willingness to forgive others. Above all else, it is for *your* benefit that you are commanded to forgive, no one else's. Don't get hung up on your enemy's getting away with an advantage over you. Forgiving is for your benefit, not your enemy's!

It has been my sad experience that many Christians who claim to have received God's forgiveness know little about forgiving others. By some strange logic they exclude anyone who has hurt them from the list of those to whom they should show love and have a forgiving attitude. I know wives who cannot forgive husbands, children their parents, and workers their bosses. We need, it seems, some training in the "art of forgiving." I have often considered running therapy groups designed to enhance our ability to forgive one another and perhaps will do this one day. I think that such training could revolutionize relationships in our homes, churches, and work situations.

The third step in handling an angry feeling is to *express the anger*. Only after the first two steps have been taken (recognizing the anger and releasing its vindictiveness through forgiveness) are you ready to take the third. This step need only be taken if the feeling of anger is still with you after you have given up vindictiveness and if it can be done constructively. If someone has angered you, it may be necessary for you to express this anger to the person concerned. It is far better to do this than to continue to harbor the unexpressed anger feeling and allow it to influence your relationship in negative ways. However, in expressing your anger there are a number of rules you should follow:

• *Try to deal with your hurts and anger as they arise, one at a time.* This may mean developing more assertiveness and courage to face those who hurt you and thus avoid allowing your hurts to accumulate. There is a danger that you may only have enough assertiveness to face the person when your anger has been turned to hostility, and once your anger has been transformed into hostility and aggression you are hardly in a good position to talk about your anger objectively.

• *Accept responsibility for your anger.* It is *your* feeling, and there is no point in trying to force the other person into accepting responsibility for it. Your anger may not even be justified and could be due to a misunderstanding. Do not blame others for your feeling without adequate reason, therefore.

• *State your hurt objectively.* Don't exaggerate. Don't generalize. And don't bring up the past. Stay current and confine your discussion to what you are experiencing now.

• *Acknowledge the right of the other person to feelings also.* He may also be hurting, and your approach to him about your anger could easily be the cause of an anger reaction in him.

• *Listen, receive, and accept any explanation or apology that may be offered.* Accept it gracefully and thankfully, but do not try to force an apology out of the other person. Your goal should be to facilitate clear communication about the nature of your anger and what is causing it.

• *Make a goal of trying to get understanding between the two of you, and not necessarily agreement.* This is probably the most difficult step for you, since you may still have some need to hurt back. Keep going back to a place of forgiveness. You may never get the other person to agree with the reason for your anger, but if you can achieve some mutual understanding, it will facilitate the resolution of your anger. Your desire should be to help clear up misunderstanding and to communicate to the other person the effect of his action on you and how this causes you to feel hurt. If you have successfully moved yourself to an attitude of forgiveness (and willingness to ask for forgiveness if you find you are also guilty), this experience should not only resolve your anger but deepen the intimacy of your relationship with the offending person.

Expressing your anger can be a very important step if you are generally not an assertive person. If you cannot easily call a halt when you are being hurt, you may need to improve your assertiveness and learn how to express your hurt feelings more directly. As I have tried to show, "turning the other cheek" has more to do with avoiding revenge than with cowardice, so don't use this as an excuse behind which to hide your lack of assertiveness.

4. When anger has become hostility.   When your anger has found expression in some hostile act or behavior, you must be honest enough to realize that you have crossed the boundary from a feeling (which is legitimate) into a behavior which has potential for sin. Your goal at this point must be to retreat—as rapidly as you can—to the feeling state and deal with it in terms of forgiveness. If you have retaliated and created hurt in another person, you should take steps to remedy this. It takes an honest and mature person to admit that he is wrong. At this point the problem is now yours—no matter how legitimate you may feel your anger is and how wrong the other person was to have done or said what he did. It is no longer the other's action that is at fault, but your reaction. The sooner you can remedy the situation by

apologizing and withdrawing your punishment or whatever else
you may be doing, the sooner you will be a free person again.

Developing a Perspective on Your Hurts

Life is full of potential for hurt and thus can create in us anger
at every turn. It is inevitable that we will be hurt by people and
by circumstance. People hurt us *because* they are human. They
make mistakes; they are selfish and self-centered; they demand
perfection and are intolerant of our mistakes—just as we are of
them! We can be hurt by circumstances over which we have no
control. We can become ill with cancer or become paralyzed in an
accident. Some circumstances can be avoided, but we are often
caught unawares and suffer the consequences. The potential for
being hurt is there all the time. If we allow these hurts to create
anger in us every time, we can hardly be free and happy. If they
get the better of us, we have to deal with both the hurts and the
anger, and we barely have the capacity to deal just with the
anger.

When unresolved anger is experienced over a period of time, it
creates in us a feeling of displeasure and indignation which is
called "resentment." This is in turn a powerful controller of other
emotions and behaviors. Resentment can create and maintain in
us such a strong feeling of revenge that it can become a grudge we
carry for a long period of time. Some people are able to carry a
grudge for their whole lives, postponing the opportunity to hurt
back almost indefinitely. These scars of resentment are un-
earthed in therapy, and I have known elderly people who have
carried resentments about their hurts from the early years of
childhood and have been unable to get rid of them. This has taken
the happiness out of their lives and caused them many years of
misery.

Carrying resentment for such a long time can easily take its
toll on your physical and mental life. It can cause ulcers, high
blood pressure, and a host of other complaints. Psychologically
these people become unattractive and difficult to relate to, develop an angry personality, and collect "hurt stamps" for a book of
grudges, hoping that the day will come when they will be able to
cash them in and satisfy all their feelings of revenge. Your re-

sentment is hard to recognize, isn't it? It eludes your awareness
and somehow remains camouflaged during those occasional attempts you make at being totally honest with yourself. Whenever
it is noticed by someone, you jump to its defense by saying, "But I
have a right to feel hurt. Look at how much emotional pain I have
suffered." It makes you sensitive and touchy. You are suspicious
of what others think and say. You are very selective in what you
listen to and distort what you hear so as to feed your hurts and
maintain your resentment. Is this how God intended you to live? I
doubt whether you can be happy like this.

To help you put your hurts, resentment, and deep urges for
revenge in proper perspective, Jesus told an important parable in
Matthew 18:21–35. It was after the Transfiguration, and He was
about to leave Galilee and move on to Capernaum and Jerusalem
where He knew He would have to face the prospect of the Cross.
Peter asked Jesus, "Lord, how often am I to forgive my brother if
he wrongs me?" Jesus then told the parable of the king who decided to settle his accounts with all his servants. One servant had
a debt of millions of dollars, so to speak. The servant, pleading for
mercy and promising to pay it all back, moved the king so much
that he forgave the servant's debt, every cent of it. This was
despite the servant's offer to pay it back over a period of time.
This servant, shortly after leaving the king, encounterd another
servant who owed him the equivalent of perhaps ten dollars and
he demanded that the debt be paid. The second servant made the
same offer as the first had made to the king, but this time it was
refused and the first servant had him jailed until the debt was
paid. This distressed everybody and they told the king what had
happened. He became furious! "I forgave you all your debt," he
said to the first servant. "Should you not have had the same
compassion on your fellow servant?"

> [Jesus ends the parable:] "And so angry was the master
> that he condemned the man to torture until he should pay the
> debt in full. And that is how my heavenly Father will deal
> with you, unless you each forgive your brother from your
> hearts.
>
> Matthew 18:34, 35 NEB

What a clear message there is in this parable. You cannot miss the essential truth of what Jesus is saying. In essence He is reminding us that we owe God more than we owe anyone else. I have caused God more hurt than any other person can ever cause me (the ratio is about 200,000 to 1, if I am to take the parable literally). If God has therefore forgiven me, what right have I not to forgive you if you hurt me? We can so easily suffer from "hurt myopia," a disorder in which we always see the hurts we cause others as being smaller than the hurts they cause us. Why not try seeing all the hurts others have caused you in the perspective of the hurts you have caused God by your waywardness and disobedience? This perspective, if you allow it to filter down to the depths of your being, can liberate you from the prison of resentment and allow you to experience and live in the freedom of an attitude which is overflowing with forgiveness. And this is all possible because He *first* forgave you.

Can Anger Accumulate?

I often hear both psychologists and lay people talking about how their anger builds up or accumulates. Implied in this idea is the belief that they need to "drain away" the anger from the past. While their terms may describe how it feels to a person when anger is experienced over a period of time, these ideas are erroneous and misleading and can even be damaging to an individual, as they can become a powerful determiner of how one handles one's anger from the past. One of my clients literally believed that all his anger went into a large reservoir and was stored up for the time when it had to be drained. This mental image so haunted him that he began to fear what would happen when his reservoir of anger became so full that it would burst. What was even more damaging was his belief that until all this anger had been allowed to find expression, he would not be free of it. He was patiently waiting for a time and opportunity when he could "pull the plug" and let it all go. Consequently, he kept alive all the memories of past hurts he had experienced and brooded over them regularly. Needless to say, this belief about the nature of his anger was more damaging to him than the anger itself.

The idea that anger can accumulate as if it were being placed in a reservoir is a common one and finds its origin in the energy theory of anger. This theory supposes that every time we get angry we build up a state of tension within ourselves, and the energy thus created is stored and must be discharged before the anger will subside. As proof that this is what happens, these theorists point to the fact that we experience relief from our anger whenever we lash out at the source of the anger. As I have tried to show, this is merely a way of transforming anger into hostility, and it is this hostility that satisfies our need to hurt back. Whenever we do this, our anger may subside. But the notion of stored anger is misleading. While it may appear that you are draining away some of your dammed-up anger when you become hostile and aggressive, this apparent relief does not prove that anything is actually stored.

I prefer to describe anger as an emotion that is always in the "here and now." This is true of all feelings and emotions. They can only exist in the present. I cannot have any anger that is left over from yesterday. To be correct, all I can say is that I have a memory of some past event that has the ability to re-create anger in me in the present. If a friend said something to me last week that was hurtful and made me extremely angry, it is not last week's anger that I am experiencing today as I reflect upon the hurt. It is the memory of the hurtful comment that continues to re-create anger in me in the present.

This idea has important implications for how you deal with your anger. It means that you don't have to deal with some hypothetically stored-up anger from the past, but rather with the power of your memories to retrigger your anger. How can you do this? Obviously you cannot forget everything hurtful that has happened to you. "Forgive and forget" is trite and simplistic, and I hope that you never give this as advice to anyone!

The solution lies not in forgetting—but in breaking the *power* of your memories to re-create the feelings of hurt at some later date. In order to do this you will have to challenge your memories. Did someone actually say what you think he said, or did you imagine it? Did this person intend to hurt you? Even so, did you cause him to do it? Could you have some other reason for feeling hurt? By carefully exploring your hurt memories in this way, you can remove their ability to bother you. Even after you have done all this, there may be some memories you can do nothing about; you will have to move yourself to the place of forgiveness. If someone has deliberately and maliciously hurt you, what else can you do but forgive? If you are not big enough for this, ask God to help you.

Jesus and Anger

I cannot close this chapter without commenting on what I believe to be an erroneous use of Jesus' anger to justify feelings of anger in ourselves. You must often hear the comment, as I do, that since Jesus got angry, it must be in order if we do. When we make such a comment we forget to make the important distinction between anger as *feeling* and anger as *hostility and aggression.* Portions of Scripture (*see* John 2:13–17; Matthew 23:13–39) which describe Jesus as getting angry are often used, in my opinion, merely to justify the perpetuation of a need to hurt someone back. This is a cover for our own hostility. Some would even go so far as to use it to justify the idea that we should get angry more frequently than we do, as if it served some purpose in cleansing our souls.

While I accept that true anger, as feeling, is legitimate and a normal response, I am strongly of the opinion that—since there is so much potential in anger for causing further hurt to all the parties concerned—it is better if we never get angry. By this I don't mean that we should deny our anger. If we could have the choice and were able to develop the ability never to experience anger, we would be much healthier persons. Those who hide behind Jesus' anger as a justification for their own fail to realize that when Jesus became angry He was totally lacking in any selfish involvement. He could get angry impartially, He always acted in the best interests of those around Him, and never had any desire for revenge or need to hurt back those who hurt Him in order to relieve His anger feelings. If He became angry, He did so in response to the hurt which people were causing themselves. Mark 3:5 makes this point clearly: "And when he had looked round about on them with anger, being grieved for the hardness of their hearts . . ." (KJV).

It is my opinion that there is no person who can be so totally free of selfish involvement and personal hurt. We all have the potential for transforming our angry feelings into hostility and aggression, and consequently we will always be potentially in need of forgiveness for our sin. This was not true of Jesus, so any attempt to draw a comparison between our anger and the anger that Jesus experienced must lead to erroneous and misleading conclusions. Jesus demonstrated to us that anger can be dealt with constructively. If we could get angry only at what Jesus got angry at, we would make a wonderful world.

Summary

If you can avoid ever getting angry, you are in a better position than if you allow yourself freely to experience anger feelings. However, if you do become angry, the feeling in itself is not harmful, provided you resolve it as soon as possible—since it has the potential for being transformed into hostility and hence sin. Knowing how to forgive others effectively by surrendering your right to hurt them back if they hurt you is the best way for resolving your anger. Whenever possible, and provided you have overcome your feelings for revenge, it is helpful to communicate your angry feelings to those who are causing them and attempt to obtain some understanding between you about the reasons for your anger.

Additional Reading

1. *The Freedom of Forgiveness.* David Augsburger. Chicago: Moody Press.
2. *The Forgiving Community.* William Klassen. Philadelphia: Westminster.
3. *Freedom From Guilt.* Bruce Narramore and Bill Counts. Irvine, California: Harvest House.
4. Matthew 5:38–48; 18:21–35.

6

Freedom From Depression

DEPRESSION IS ONE of the most complicated of all our emotions. It is complicated because it usually involves other emotions as well, and because it can range in intensity from a mild feeling of the blues to one of the severest of all mental disorders requiring hospitalization. Since depression is the major cause of suicide, it cannot be ignored. It is also the most commonly experienced unpleasant emotion and inflicts itself upon all of us at some time or another in our lives, with a large percentage of the population experiencing some depression as a daily occurrence. Interest in the problem of depression has risen sharply over the last decade, especially since it appears that more people are suffering from depression than ever before. This is, I believe, a reflection on the life-styles we are developing in our western culture and the general loss of meaning and purpose in life that many are experiencing. The more affluent and secure we have become, the more boredom we experience and the more prone we are to seeking ways of escape through drugs and alcohol (which are the most common forms of self-treatment for depression). Whatever our station in life and regardless of our age or sex, none of us can claim to be totally free of depression. Some, fortunately, do not experience it as often as others, and many who claim to be depression free are probably just not able to recognize its symptoms.

96 FEELING FREE

A Timeless, Universal Problem

It can be most comforting to realize that depression is as old as the human race. There is ample evidence to show that ever since the beginning of human history, mankind has experienced depression. It appears to be built into our system and, as we will see later, serves a very important protective function. The first clear clinical description of depression comes to us from Hippocrates in the fourth century B.C., and the description sounds like an extract from a modern textbook on abnormal psychology. Hippocrates gives prominence to problems of love as a cause of depression, and both the Greeks and Romans held the view that all depression was caused by disappointments in love. Our teenage population might very well agree with this analysis!

The Bible also gives at least two clear descriptions of depression. In the story of King Ahab (1 Kings 21), when he could not have Naboth's vineyards, we are told that King Ahab ". . . turned away his face, and would eat no bread " (v. 4 KJV). He displayed the typical signs of severe depression when he could not get his way—and this pattern has not changed at all these thousands of years. And then there was Elijah the Prophet who had had such a victory on Mount Carmel (1 Kings 18). He prayed, and fire came down and consumed his offering, an obvious sign that God was on his side. He prayed again, and it rained. When it was all finished he ran for his life into the wilderness and was overcome by a deep depression. He sat under a juniper tree and prayed that God would let him die (1 Kings 19:4). Here we see a very common reaction which often follows periods of extreme elation or exhilaration. The depressing effects of an anticlimax are well known to all of us. Merely accepting this as a normal physiological reaction to overactivity can free one to take full advantage of the depression in order to allow one's body to recover.

Not only has depression always been with us, but it is also a universal phenomenon. Go to any part of the world and, wherever you find people, no matter what their cultural history, you will find the experience of depression. It may take on slightly different forms, but you cannot mistake what it is. I was born and raised in

Africa as a European and was exposed to many primitive cultures as well as to groups which were experiencing transition to a western culture. In the more primitive groups, the element of guilt is notably absent from their depression. The tendency in these cultures is for blame for disaster to be externalized and placed on evil forces or ancestors. People tend, therefore, not to blame themselves for everything that happens and, surprisingly, this has important implications for their mental health. As one observes the transition to a western culture, blame gradually becomes self-directed (Who else *can* you blame?) and a strong tendency towards guilt develops. Consequently, there is a much greater guilt component in the depressions of those in a western-type culture. With or without the guilt component, depression is universal, and the problem is not so much how to avoid it as what to do with it when it comes.

A Word of Caution

At the outset I need to stress very strongly that there are many forms of depression. Some are very obviously caused by physical factors such as poor sleeping or eating habits and fatigue, while others are due to biochemical disturbances or genetic factors. The discussion in this chapter will focus primarily on those depressions that are psychological in nature. If you (or someone you know) are experiencing a prolonged or severe depression with serious immobilization and extensive loss of perspective—or if there is preoccupation with suicide—I would recommend that you seek immediate professional help. Some forms of depression need special treatment, including the use of anti-depressant medication, and one should not delay obtaining treatment simply because of a fear of drug addiction or the like. Under proper care there is little risk of this happening, and there is no point in living a miserable life when help can be obtained so easily. Our popularization of antidrug feelings is causing many severely depressed people to avoid seeking appropriate help, a most unfortunate trend, since the medication involved is not addictive in the traditional sense. If you have weak eyes, you don't hesitate to use corrective glasses. If you have a biochemical or genetic predisposition towards depression, you should feel as much freedom in correcting the defect with medication as you would about wearing glasses.

What Do We Know About Depression?

We are beset by theories about depression which range from seeing all depression as purely psychological to those which see the problem as entirely physiological. Most likely the truth lies somewhere between these two extremes, and most depressions can be seen as an interaction between psychological and physiological factors. Any theory that is going to be helpful will have to take into consideration this interactive process. Sometimes it is a psychological factor that triggers the depression, but since our minds and bodies operate in unison, this depression must be seen as being more than merely the set of ideas we have in our heads. These ideas and thoughts have caused our bodies to respond in a certain way, producing changes in our glands, stomach, respiration, heartbeat, and so on, which—together with the thoughts—constitute the total depressed package. This is why very often we find that if we have experienced some deep depression, the emotion does not go away the moment the cause for the depression has disappeared. The disturbed body chemistry which resulted from the depression will require a period of time to pass before a proper balance can be restored. I am stressing this because I frequently find that people who are depression prone have not understood how it is that their bodies interact with their minds. A person might say to me, "Oh, I was so depressed this morning, but even though the cause has gone I am still feeling depressed."

"When did the cause go away?" I might ask.

"Well, just over an hour ago!" is the reply. It is unreasonable to expect that one's physiology should return to normal so quickly. The speed with which your system returns to normal will depend on a number of factors, including the depth of the depression (the deeper the depression, the longer it will take for your system to recover); the nature of your own physiology (some of us have systems that require a longer period of time to recover than others); whether there are distracting factors (if you are recovering from a depression and find yourself taken up with some other engaging activity, you are likely to recover more rapidly than if your activity is not distracting).

The implication of all of this is that you must come to understand and accept your particular and unique style of recovery from depression and learn how to adjust and make allowance for it. Find ways of distracting yourself during the recovery period, such as getting into a good book or hobby, and your return to normal feelings will take place more rapidly. It will also avoid the possibility of your reacting to your feelings during the recovery period and causing yourself to precipitate further depression.

The cyclic nature of our emotions.   Before exploring the problem of depression in depth, I need to draw your attention to the normal cyclical pattern of our emotions. It is possible that some of my readers may believe that they are depression prone when all they are experiencing is a normal low in their emotional cycle.

Physiological research has repeatedly shown us that emotions have a tendency to be cyclical in nature and that we each have our own characteristic cycle of emotionality. Periods of good feelings (elation) are followed by periods of bad feelings (depression), and these can repeat themselves over and over again under the influence of hormonal or other cycles. Some people do not experience much variability, while others experience so much variation that the lows may be severe enough to incapacitate them. These cycles are often misunderstood or misinterpreted, and the misunderstanding about the consequences can be the cause of more unpleasantness than the low feeling itself.

These cycles must be accepted as normal and largely outside the control of the person experiencing them. They are obviously caused by involuntary physiological rhythms. The menstrual cycle in women is one type of biological rhythm which influences emotional life, and while I do not believe in the simplistic views of the proponents of "biorhythms" as popularly presented, there is enough evidence to show that biological cycles are present to some degree and that they can influence our emotions. They cannot be predicted as easily as the biorhythms which theorists suggest, as the cycles are not fixed and constant but may vary just as does the menstrual cycle of women. Fatigue, illness, virus invasions of the body, and so on all influence these cycles, so there is no way you can predict them with any accuracy. You should, however, come to know your own characteristic cycle and learn how to "mark time" or slow down when you are in a low or depressed period and wait until your normal feelings and judgment return. When you are in a high state and feel elated, savor it, use it to good advantage, and accomplish those difficult tasks that are waiting to be done. Don't get angry at yourself or another person for what happens during a high or low period. Do not trust your feelings of depression and allow yourself to feel suicidal or wanting to run away from life's difficulties, just because your cycle has caught you in a low period. Many suicides, decisions for divorce, and resignations from jobs occur during these biological low periods and they are regretted afterwards.

Depression as a symptom and a reaction. There are many forms of depression. The low described in the previous section is more a biological than a psychological depression. What we more typically label "depression" is that mood which is triggered or maintained by psychological factors and is accompanied by an extensive loss of perspective and distortion of reality. Other symptoms of depression are loss of appetite, loss of interest in one's surroundings, lethargy, self-criticism and condemnation, and overwhelming feelings of unworthiness.

But depression is both a symptom and a reaction. As a *symptom* it can be a warning signal that something needs attention. Its function here is one of preservation, and it is designed to slow you down and disengage you from your environment. You lose interest in what you are doing, you withdraw from your contacts, and you may even want to withdraw from life. This allows your system time to recover and prevents any further damage being caused from overexertion.

Depression can also be a symptom accompanying infections, as occurs during influenza, or it can be part of a disease state, as when it is seen in thyroid disorders and cancer. The greatest mistake one can make when experiencing these sorts of depression is to search for reasons for them in your environment and then to blame these for the depression. If you accuse your wife or yell at the children or blame your job for your depression, you may be doing a great injustice. Your depression may simply be a symptom of your physical disturbance.

But depression is also a *reaction* to your life's experiences. It has to do with the way you deal with your environment and this is why these depressions are often called "reactive." They occur in response to the way you receive and handle life's blows. At this point I should distinguish between *reactive* and *neurotic* depressions. While many psychologists believe that all reactive depressions are neurotic, I prefer to make a distinction between the two. It is possible to experience a frequent depressive reaction to some event, without its being characterized as neurotic. This latter label is reserved for a much more pervasive and elusive life-style, where one takes on all of life with a depressed mood. It is more a way of dealing with deep-seated anxiety than anything else. If you consider yourself to be this way, I strongly recommend that you seek professional help. The depressive reactions which are discussed in this chapter are not continuous in character but tend to come in spurts as a reaction to some life event. They eventually disappear, although they may have been the cause of considerable pain at the time.

Depression as a response to loss.   I believe that the key to understanding nearly all of the reactive depressions is to see them as a response to a sense of loss. If you can come to understand how this sense of loss is triggered—and develop ways for evaluating the loss and dealing with its reality—you can learn to overcome these depressions. I have found the technique I will be describing extremely effective for myself as well as for clients, and you should find it easy to implement in your own life.

There are four types of losses which can trigger depressions: real losses, abstract losses, imagined losses, and threatened losses. A clear understanding of the distinction between them can facilitate early recognition of your particular loss whenever you experience depression.

1. REAL LOSSES: These are the easiest to identify, although in some instances it is possible to be so depressed that you fail to give attention to the preceding events. This includes the loss of a

real object, as when you have misplaced some prized object, or the loss of (or mere separation from) someone you love very much. I have experienced depressions ranging in severity from a mild low to where I have been extremely miserable, as I am sure you have, in response to losses such as dropping and breaking my camera, receiving a speeding ticket (where the loss was both the money wasted on the fine as well as the loss of my self-esteem), and when I first had to start wearing reading glasses (which represented the loss of some prized faculty). These are all *real losses* because they are tangible in form and can be felt or measured in some way. The list of real losses can be very long! Since we are tied to a material world, it is inevitable that we will experience many such losses over and over again. If we are tied too much to this world, we will be prone to experience real loss much more deeply than others, and the success with which we can deal with our depressions will depend to a great extent on our ability to develop a proper perspective on worldly things. I will discuss this further when we look at the Christian's resources for dealing with depression, but it is my strong conviction that a religious orientation can help here considerably.

2. ABSTRACT LOSSES: Some losses are not real and tangible and cannot be weighed or measured. They are more abstract in nature, but this does not make them any less powerful as triggers of depression. *Abstract losses* can include the loss of love (when you are jilted by a lover), the loss of self-respect (when you are criticized by a friend or your boss), the loss of hope or ambition (when your application is rejected by a graduate school), or the loss of being needed (when you are retired from your employment and/or when your children all finally leave home and start their independent lives). Some of us experience a loss of power or prestige whenever someone else "equals" us through promotion or through the development of extra skills. These losses may be very abstract, but as far as their ability to trigger depression is concerned, they are equally as powerful as any real losses we suffer. In one respect they are more difficult to deal with, as they often are much more elusive and hard to identify. They represent such vague and unquantifiable needs that it requires careful thought and often professional help to break the recognition barrier. Let

me stress that it is absolutely essential, if you are going to overcome depression, to train yourself in identifying the abstract
losses you experience.

3. IMAGINED LOSSES: Sometimes our imagination runs away
with us. We find ourselves brooding over some incident and very
soon we have conjured up a thought that has no factual backing.
This *imagined loss* can then trigger a depression. Perhaps we
imagine that we have been snubbed, ridiculed, or rejected (all
forms of loss of pride), or we become suspicious that a spouse is
betraying us by being unfaithful. Paranoid thoughts like these
can be a major cause of ongoing depression, since we are set up to
imagine all sorts of losses. Since these losses are only imagined, it
is ridiculous to allow them to make you unhappy.

In order to deal with imagined losses, you should concentrate
on testing the reality of your imagined fears. It may be that what
you fear has some basis in reality, but most times your imagination has had a field day and played havoc with you. Force yourself
to see your thoughts only as imaginations and, if necessary, check
them out by asking the right questions or carefully weighing up
the odds of your imagination being correct. If you are in doubt—
forget it!

4. THREATENED LOSSES: A depression may be caused simply by
a threatened loss. No actual loss may have occurred or need
necessarily occur. The threat alone is sufficient to trigger the
depression. As with the other types, *threatened losses* can be just
as depression producing as an actual loss. Have you not taken
someone who is close to you to the hospital for minor surgery and
found yourself somewhat depressed? You wait patiently with a
knot in your stomach and all need for food gone. Your head tells
you that the risk of death in the surgical procedure is very low. No
actual loss has taken place, but the threat of loss is sufficient to
cause you to experience depression.

We are bombarded in life with threats. We are threatened with
the loss of a job, a spouse, a reputation, some opportunity to make
money, and these can cause a reaction of depression just as easily
as if some actual loss had occurred. Often it can be worse, since
threatened losses have a much greater ability to play on our
imaginations than real losses. The depressive response to real

losses is often called "grief," and while the pain in the grief process may be unpleasant, it usually is "time limited" as we can better test the reality of these losses. The effect of imagined or threatened losses can drag us on indefinitely and produce much more psychological damage than real losses.

Dealing With Depression

List your losses. It can be helpful if you take a moment to prepare a list of those losses you have experienced recently or that you find yourself experiencing repeatedly. Categorize them as real, abstract, imagined, or threatened. Examine your marriage, your job, school life, family life, recreation, goals, and accomplishments and see how many losses of the various types you can identify. Recollect every depression experience you have ever had and try to identify the loss, no matter how small or subtle. Often one event can be the cause of many subtle minor losses. This exercise can alert you to repeated tendencies to experience loss and give you some perspective on how you value things, how you set yourself up for unrealistic expectation, and how frequently you distort the severity of the loss. You should come to realize that life still goes on and seems to provide many substitutes for those things we lose. If this is so, then why not reduce the impact of these losses?

Recognize psychological factors. Whether the loss is real, abstract, imagined, or only threatened, psychological factors play an important role in precipitating and perpetuating depression, as they do in all the emotions. Obviously, *awareness* of the loss is a necessary first step. Losses don't affect us while we are asleep. It is only when we awaken and become aware of the loss that we experience a reaction such as depression. This has an important bearing on the mechanism that precipitates our depression and gives the clue to how we should handle it. You see, it is not the loss *per se* that causes the depression, but our *interpretation* of the loss. It is what the loss means to us in terms of our values, beliefs, and expectations that determines how we will react. This means that if we can get our values sorted out, put our expectations in realistic perspective, and have a right attitude to life, we can reduce both the frequency and pain of our depressions, shorten their duration, and even avoid them altogether in many situations. I know, because I've done it myself!

Psychological factors also play an important role in *perpetuating* depression. As we will see shortly when I discuss the depression cycle, depressions often perpetuate themselves. If what we believe about a loss (and say to ourselves concerning it) triggers a depression, continuing to believe and say these things to oneself can perpetuate it. You may very well have been snubbed by a friend or rejected for some job and consequently experienced a depressive reaction. If you continue to say to yourself, "Nobody cares for me," or "I am never going to be able to get a decent job that satisfies me," you will perpetuate the depression and prolong it unnecessarily. You may even intensify the depression and increase your emotional pain.

The Depression Cycle

The ideal way to resolve a depression is to allow yourself to experience the sadness of the loss as deeply as possible. Do your grieving thoroughly. Neither short-circuit the grief process nor oppose the depression in either yourself or anyone else. This will only prolong it. The greatest mistake we can make when giving advice to someone who is depressed is to say to them, "Come on now; snap out of it. You don't have to be so depressed." We usually have a need to say this because *we* are experiencing some discomfort as a result of their depression. This advice is callous, ineffective, and often just intensifies the depression, as it represents a further loss because of your implied rejection.

We must accept that if a legitimate loss has been experienced, it is normal and even necessary that the person experiencing the loss must grieve over it appropriately. This is as true when the loss is real (as through the death of a spouse) as it is for any other type of loss. The depression in this case serves a very valuable and protective function and—provided it is not perpetuated unnecessarily—helps the person to evaluate and come to terms with the loss. This "ideal" depression cycle is depicted in Figure 4.

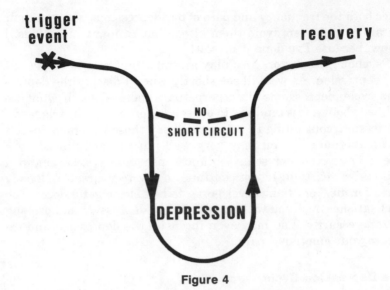

Figure 4

The "Ideal" Depression Response

Note that the "trigger" of the depression is the awareness and evaluation of the loss—and the depth of the depression will be determined by the significance of the loss. If the cycle is not short-circuited, the person will begin to recover from the depression after a while and then continue with his life, having placed the loss in some new evaluative category. Unfortunately, we don't always follow this ideal pattern. What happens more typically is the cycle shown in Figure 5.

Here, the loss triggers the depression cycle as before, but as soon as the person begins to experience the depression he has other reactions not unlike the emotional chaining I have already described. The person may react by becoming disappointed or even disgusted with himself for responding the way he did and may even become angry at himself for allowing it to happen. The combination of anger and depression is very common, since the loss that triggers the depression can also set up a state of frustra-

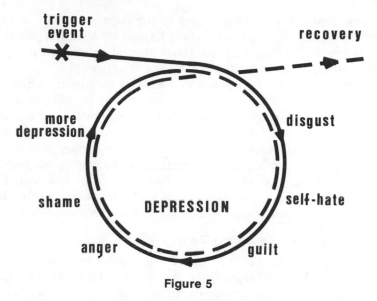

Figure 5

The Typical Depression Cycle

tion. These additional feelings, together with the general state of depression, create feelings of guilt and shame, especially if those around begin to send messages like: "Don't tell me you're depressed again!" or "Come on now; you've got nothing to be depressed about." "I don't want to be near you if you are depressed!" is probably what crowns it all, even if these words are not actually verbalized. In our depressed condition we can be very sensitive to the body language and attitudes of those around us. The end result of all of this is a deeper sense of loss to which the person responds with more depression—thus perpetuating the cycle. I call this the "depression cycle," as it can repeat itself over and over again, each round augmenting the next, until it eventually loses its momentum with the passage of time and everything returns to normal. Occasionally the intensity of the depression increases and reaches serious proportions. The secondary losses we experience whenever we react to our depression can be very subtle and depend largely for their impact on how accepting we are of our depression, whether those around us are accepting or condemning of us, and whether we are anger prone.

This circularity of depression can account for why insignificant losses can trigger very deep depressions or why we hold on to our depressions for a long time. The healthiest way to deal with loss is to make sure that you experience an "appropriate" amount of depression. You can overcome the depression more rapidly by avoiding the trap of secondary reactions and allowing yourself to be depressed by not condemning yourself for how you feel. The initial loss is enough to care about without creating a further sense of loss which is only a consequence of the depression.

How to Avoid Perpetuating Depression

The steps you need to take in order to resolve a depression and avoid prolonging or intensifying it are not too difficult to implement. At first it may require a little discipline and deliberate application, but once you have found how successful the technique can be, you will discover that it takes much less effort to abort depression than it does to perpetuate it. There are six steps:

1. Learn to recognize your depressions. It seems so obvious, doesn't it? However, very often we do not bring our feeling of depression into our conscious awareness. We may not notice it until someone else draws attention to it. Contract with people close to you to tell you whenever they think you are depressed. Don't deny or fight their opinion, and certainly don't take it as criticism. If you experience depression often, it may be easier for you to catch yourself and admit this feeling to yourself. Sometimes depression is hidden behind feelings of despondency, lethargy, anger, or plain unhappiness. If you find yourself lacking energy, losing interest in all your activities, feeling that life has no future, you will certainly be experiencing depression. Admit it and label it as such to yourself.

2. Don't fight or resist your depression. Since depression is legitimate, it must be experienced up to a point. Fighting or resisting it only intensifies your secondary reactions to the depression, since in most cases you will not win over it. Don't blame others for it—force yourself to accept the idea that it is both normal and necessary that you allow yourself to be depressed. The more effective you are in doing this, the quicker you will recover from the depression.

3. Identify the loss that triggered the depression. Was it real, abstract, imagined, or threatened? This may be easy to do on some occasions but hard on others, since the loss may be very subtle and elusive. Talk it over with a friend and see whether you can develop some insight. Examine past experiences that may be similar and see whether you can identify a trend or theme in your reactions. Don't play down the importance of little things. Our emotions don't always respond to logical or rational perceptions, and often very small or innocuous things can trigger deep feelings of loss below our level of awareness. Their power to do this may be related to experiences from our early life when responses were conditioned to these ideas or words, and we may no longer have any recollection of the association.

4. Face the reality of the loss. If our loss is real, the quicker we can move to accepting the reality of the loss, the better. We have a tendency always to deny loss and avoid facing the reality of a situation, creating irrational hopes in ourselves that the loss will be restored. We are also very selective in the information we choose to perceive. "I won't believe it. It's just not true!" is a common reaction to severe loss, such as the death of someone close to you—but such denial only prolongs the pain.

In most cases, facing the reality of the loss inevitably means accepting the irreversibility of the situation. There are some things in life that cannot be changed, and to engage in wishful thinking that they will does not change anything. Forcing yourself to accept the loss is the only way you can go forward and heal your emotions.

If the loss is not real but only imagined, your strategy must be to confront your fears. Check out whether your imagination has any foundation, by seeking information that will clarify your situation. If, for example, you imagine that a friend is angry with

you and you experience this as a loss, go to the friend and clarify
the relationship. If your friend is really angry, your loss is real
and not imagined and can be dealt with accordingly. If he or she is
not, you are only wasting your emotional energy. In general, the
principle here is to try to convert all your imagined losses to real
ones wherever this can be done. Accept the reality of these losses
and discard all the remaining imagined ones. You will be surprised at how many of your imagined fears and losses have no
grounds in reality whatsoever and can be discarded. All it takes is
a little effort in checking them out.

5. Develop a perspective on your loss.   We tend to react to
everything as if it were catastrophic. Perhaps you have received a
letter from a friend who expresses anger toward you. It seems as if
life has stopped, and nothing else matters at that moment. A
cloud hangs over you the rest of the day. But then something else
happens that eclipses the earlier loss. Let's say you have a car
accident and injure someone. You feel very badly, so much so that
the early problem now seems insignificant. Why? Because the
later and more serious problem has altered your perspective on
the earlier incident. If you could only develop the ability to put
your losses in their proper perspective and see them in the context
of larger issues, you could save yourself a lot of misery. Why wait
until something really catastrophic happens before you do this?
The old-fashioned idea of counting your many blessings whenever
faced with tragedy may not be such a bad idea after all!

My wife and I, during our early twenties, ran a small Sunday
school and conducted church services in a poor area of our city
every week. On a day when we were very depressed over our
financial situation, particularly because we could not upgrade the
standard of our automobile, we went visiting some of the
parishioners. It wasn't long before we came across a family where
the husband was an alcoholic and had not been home for months.
On the morning of our visit, the wife (a mother of three children)
had been told by her doctor that she had developed breast cancer.
What do you think happened to our depression over our financial
situation? We wondered what the woman was feeling, so I asked
her. Can you imagine my reaction when she told us that she was

so thankful that the illness had not come earlier in her life when her children were smaller and could not take care of themselves! Now, at least, if anything happened to her, they could care for themselves. She had put everything in the best perspective she knew, and I learned the lesson that no matter how bad my situation might be, it could always be worse. So why not be thankful for it as it is? We need always to put our catastrophes in that perspective. When viewed in this way, some of our losses become petty and insignificant and don't deserve the attention we give them. If they *are* serious, let us have the courage to face them realistically.

6. *Learn from your depression.* We can avoid many depressions if we learn from our past experiences. Often we will find ourselves repeating the same depression over and over again because we fail to realize that it is the same trigger that causes it. We set ourselves up to experience a loss by believing or expecting something to happen and experience loss because it doesn't. I know of many marriages where either the husband or the wife sets up unrealistic expectations. The wife may expect her husband to be polite on all occasions, or the husband may expect his wife to have dinner ready when he comes home from work. These expectations, while they are desirable, are often unnecessary and result from unclear communication. It follows that these expectations are not always met, and consequently a loss is repeatedly experienced and becomes the trigger for anger and depression.

You can deal with these unmet expectations by improving your communication skills. Make sure that you get agreement on what you want—or drop your expectations! Since many of your expectations are not going to be satisfied anyway, why hang on to them? If you don't expect your husband to be polite and he is, this is a bonus. If he isn't, nothing is lost. It never ceases to amaze me what an impact it has on relationships when I teach those involved to drop their unnecessary expectations for each other and to start viewing everything they would like to happen as a bonus. Try it and see what a difference it makes. I have a sign in my office that says BLESSED ARE THEY THAT EXPECT NOTHING, FOR THEY'LL GET EVERYTHING. The real impact of this attitude is that it reflects appreciation for what does come in life and avoids creating resentment over what doesn't.

Expectations that have mutual agreement and are clearly communicated are obviously permissible; but be careful of what you do with your disappointments.

The Christian's Resources for Dealing With Depression

This chapter would not be complete if I did not draw attention to the unique resources that are available to the Christian believer in dealing with depression. A life of faith does not automatically guarantee that one will never react to loss with depression, and this must be seen as a part of your normal defense system. You should accept the depression as a natural reaction, but then be careful with what you do with it. It is what we *do* with our depression that determines whether we are living the life of faith or failing to use the provisions that God has given us.

What are these resources? In one sense they are unlimited, but for the purpose of discussion here I want to draw your attention to three important aspects of these resources:

1. God gives perspective for our lives. Knowing God through Christ *must make a difference* to the way we view life. It should provide a vantage point from which we can evaluate our losses and help interpret our future. It forces us to constantly sort out the essentials from the nonessentials in life. If we can separate the temporal from the eternal, we should be able to sort out our values and more intelligently place an emphasis on that which is important to God.

Our attitude to money, our possessions, our accomplishments, and our ambitions must all be influenced by this perspective. If we can say, "This is a nonessential in my life, so what difference does it make if I lose it?" whenever we experience a loss, our perception of this loss must make a difference. We should be able to bring ourselves to the point of accepting loss much more readily without putting up such a fight.

Many of us could probably benefit from a weekly devotional exercise in which we put God's perspective back into our lives. Can you imagine what this could do for us if we did it regularly?

2. God gives power in our lives. The concept of Christian power has been bandied about so much that it has become a cliché without meaning. However, I believe that the idea that God can come to us in our frailty and weakness and provide us with extra resources for dealing with life's circumstances is central to the Gospel's message. We are not left to our own meager resources and do not have to struggle by ourselves. When we do reach the end of everything we can do for ourselves and cannot cope anymore—when the burden of the loss we are experiencing is just too heavy for us to carry—we can call on God for help. His help is available all along the way, and probably our most common failing is that we wait so long before we call.

3. Prayer. I am convinced that few Christians adequately tap the prayer resources that are available to them. Most praying has, unfortunately, deteriorated into a string of requests which we repeat over and over again. Prayer is provided for *our* benefit. God does not "need" our prayers in the same sense that we do. Using prayer intelligently (and by this I mean that we become absolutely authentic and honest with God) cannot leave us unchanged. It is one of the most powerful therapeutic forces I know. There is no psychotherapist more unconditional in accepting you, nor psychoanalyst more insightful in understanding your deep motivations, than your Creator. Why not let Him do some therapy with you? Your depression proneness, as well as many other emotional problems, may be resolved this way.

Summary

The experience of depression is inevitable in our lives. Most reactive depressions are a response to a sense of loss, whether this loss is real, abstract, imagined, or only threatened. Resolving depression involves identifying and accepting the reality of the loss, determining if it is real or abstract, testing the reality of imagined or threatened losses, and allowing yourself to grieve over your loss. We can avoid unnecessarily perpetuating a depression by paying attention to our self-talk and being careful about how we react to the depression. By placing our losses in proper perspective, especially if we have a Christian view of life's purpose, we can more easily accept the reality of the loss.

Paul tells us what should be our attitude to the nonessentials of life:

> But what things were gain to me, those I counted loss for Christ. Yea doubtless, and I count all things but loss for the excellency of the knowledge of Christ Jesus my Lord: for whom I have suffered the loss of all things . . . .
>
> Philippians 3:7, 8 KJV

How could you possibly be depression prone when you allow such an attitude to permeate your whole being?

Additional Reading

1. *Up From Depression*. Leonard Cammer. New York: Simon & Schuster.
2. *Depression and the Body*. Alexander Lowen. New York: Penguin.
3. *The Book of Hope: How Women Can Overcome Depression*. Helen DeRosis and Victoria Y. Pellegrino. New York: Macmillan.
4. Psalm 42.

7

Freedom From Self-Hate

"I DIDN'T KNOW who I was, but for the first time I realized I was valuable to somebody."

That's all I heard her say, yet suddenly I could piece together a complete life story. At first I could not see her, since her voice came from in front of me as I stood in line at the bank. Three or four persons separated her from me. The words rang once again through my head: ". . . for the first time I realized I was valuable to somebody."

Then I saw her. She was a dwarf, a grotesque midget. Her short arms and legs and large head drew attention to her easily. I guessed her age to be about twenty-five, and while everyone was staring at her she was quite oblivious of the attention she was getting. The woman she was talking to was tall and attractive, and the conversation quite obviously centered around some recent event in her life.

My mind raced as I pieced together her probable life story. I could imagine how resentment had built up within her at the chance misfortune that had created her a dwarf—unusual, abnormal. She was an object to be gawked at. From the earliest years of her life she would have felt "different." She saw her friends grow tall while she remained short and awkward, and this must have been very painful for her. Most of the time she would just want to hide away. She would fear going into public places and—worst of all—the patronizing way people would talk to her!

She was telling her friend how she had become a Christian six months before. For the first time she had experienced unconditional love and acceptance from God through Christ. At last she felt she was valuable enough to somebody else and now had begun to see some value in herself.

An unusual story? No, I think this is to some extent the story of us all.

What Is Your Self-Image?

"Who am I?" is a question which haunts us throughout our lives. We ask this question because within each of us there lurks a midget we hate—perhaps many midgets. There are aspects about every one of us that we dislike intensely, even hate. We fear that we have not grown up in every part of our being and begin finding ways early in life to hide those parts of ourselves we perceive as inadequate, for fear that when others see our midgets they will be repulsed.

What are the personal midgets we fear most often? Surprisingly, while people have very personalized inadequacies, most of these center around two major themes: intelligence and appearance. One does not have to look for the reasons for this. Our culture clearly prescribes which personal attributes are most prized. If you are going to succeed in life, as we have structured it, you either have to be intelligent or look beautiful. If you have neither quality, you are in trouble!

But here we see a paradox. While there are many people who are both intelligent and attractive, these qualities are only relative, and some feel that they will never meet society's standards. There is always someone more intelligent or more attractive to cause them to be dissatisfied with themselves. And so the midgets of inadequate intellect and appearance continually erode their feelings of self-worth.

Do you remember the story about the children of Israel when they had been brought out of Egypt and were on their way to the Land of Promise? As they came near to Canaan, God instructed Moses to send men to spy out the land. After a while the spies returned, but their reports were conflicting. Some said that what they saw was a land flowing with milk and honey and that although the people were strong they could be overcome. Other spies reported differently: "And there we saw the giants . . . and we were in our own sight as grasshoppers . . ." (Numbers 13:33 KJV). Giants! The problem for us is that when our self-evaluation spies come back after having searched the depths of our beings and reported that there are too many midgets, we do not have the strength to go forward. No giants, only midgets. This is the problem of low self-esteem or self-hate.

It is interesting to realize that the Apostle Paul has given us a clear prescription for dealing with our personal midgets. In psychological language it is a prescription for developing a healthy self-esteem. While he addresses more directly the problem of an *inflated* self-image (too many giants), I believe the principles are the same if the problem is self-hate (too many midgets):

> . . . do not be conceited or think too highly of yourself; but *think* your way to a *sober estimate* based on the measure of faith that God has dealt to each of you.
>
> Romans 12:3 NEB; italics added

Paul never addresses himself directly to the problem of low self-esteem (which appears to be a problem more characteristic of our age than his). Some psychologists feel that an epidemic of inferiority is raging through our society. There are more midgets than giants in the land! In some ways these midgets have always been with us, but what we are experiencing as a phenomenon of twentieth-century western culture is quite unique, as if something has gone wrong with our cultural genetics. The reasons for this are not hard to find: Our highly industrialized, computerized, and depersonalized society appears to be breeding a mass disillusionment which in turn can become the main cause for low self-esteem. There are very few new frontiers for us to conquer, and challenges are available only to a few highly specialized intellectuals. The rest must be content with being carried along like a railroad coach in the middle of a train that knows neither where it has been nor where it is going. It just follows the rest of the coaches! With no sense of destiny, no idea of purpose or sense of value to life, it is no wonder that many begin to feel like the midget: of no value to anybody.

Self-image as the basis for self-esteem. In the last decade there has been an increased focus on self-consciousness and self-scrutiny which has come about through certain branches of psychology. As human beings we have the ability to engage in self-reflection, and this forms the basis of self-image. Out of our evaluation of this self-image we develop a sense of self-esteem in which we feel either good or bad about what we see. Our evaluation of ourselves depends to a great extent on our values and belief system. While there is a danger that we can come to over-value ourselves (conceit)—the problem which Paul addresses—given our cultural milieu, the chances are much greater that we will develop a preponderance of self-hate. To develop an adequate self-esteem, it is often sufficient to merely stop hating yourself.

Closely related to the area of self-esteem is the idea of *loving yourself*. In response to a scribe who wanted to know which was the first and therefore most important commandment, Jesus replied: "And thou shalt love the Lord thy God with all thy heart, and with all thy soul, and with all thy mind, and with all thy strength . . ." (Mark 12:30 KJV). Almost immediately thereafter He added that there was a second commandment: "Thou shalt love thy neighbour as thyself" (v. 31). There were no other commandments greater than these. Loving your neighbor as yourself implies that there is a form of self-love or self-valuing that is both appropriate and a necessary prerequisite to relating effectively to other people.

If you are going to be able to value others, you must first be able to see something of value in yourself. If you do not love (in the truest sense of the word) and value yourself, you will be unable to value others.

Some Christian writers have questioned whether self-love is biblical. Did Jesus really mean that we should love our neighbor as ourselves *as a command,* or was He merely saying in effect, "You already love yourself too much and you should therefore love your neighbor just as much"? In other words, is Jesus presupposing self-love—or is He commanding it? There is no doubt in my mind that Jesus is addressing Himself primarily to the error of misunderstanding the term *neighbor,* and that He presupposes self-love. Paul does the same in Ephesians 5:28 when he tells us to love our wives as our own bodies. In neither case is self-love condemned, however, and the difficulty we have with understanding it today is more a problem with what it means to *love* than anything else.

We fear self-love because we equate it quite erroneously with pride and self-seeking. We cannot see the connection between feeling good about ourselves and yet having a sense of our sinfulness.

The misunderstanding comes from confusing one's personhood with the self-centeredness which is an expression of one's lower or sinful nature. I may be sinful by nature and selfish by disposition, but this does not mean that all of my personhood is rotten. It is my deeds, my meager attempts to win God's favor through works, that are as filthy rags in His sight, not the essence of my being. Why else would He have died for me?

Furthermore, we should not equate self-love with self-aggrandizement. To have an adequate self-esteem based on self-love, it is necessary to have an accurate self-image. We must know who and what we are, and no defects must be hidden from our view. At the same time we must have an honesty to acknowledge our strengths. How else could we use our talents for God? On the other side, I believe that a healthy self-esteem is characterized by humility, not by self-abasement and self-hate. Pride is usually an attempt to exaggerate one's giants in order to conceal one's midgets—the pursuit of self-aggrandizement, with a refusal to accept God's judgment on the inadequacy of our best deeds as a way of earning His forgiveness. Humility is characterized by an accurate self-appraisal of both strengths and weaknesses—and a willingness to accept inadequacies. This is self-love and this leads to healthy self-esteem. It is consistent with the recognition of our basic sinfulness and a willingness to receive God's grace.

It is specifically at this point that the Christian Gospel can provide us with an answer to the problem of low self-esteem. Without God we are left to struggle with our own flaws and inadequacies, to scrape together from our failures and imperfections some semblance of self-respect. By engaging in massive denial and rejection of the opinions of others, we may at best build a pseudo self-esteem which has as its superstructure flimsy beams of self-distortion and fragile supports of self-confidence. The façade of this pseudo self-esteem is merely a camouflage for the lurking midgets we hate.

The consequences of low self-esteem.   The consequences of self-hate are obvious. Its influence is like a cancer, both in the individual and in society. Low self-esteem breeds depression and even anger. Many who lack adequate assertiveness do so because they do not feel valuable enough to present their claims and assert their rights. Self-hate breeds judgmentalism and criticism and affects our interpersonal relationships in many ways. It permeates every aspect of our lives, and even Christian communities are not free from its consequences.

Perhaps the most unfortunate consequence of self-hate is that we develop a phony façade. As we go through childhood we learn ways to defend ourselves against psychological pain. Since we don't want to be hurt by the rejection of others, we withdraw and build shells of self-concealment. These phony façades are of two types. In one we set about magnifying our giants, using, of course, distortion and exaggeration. We distort our self-image by ignoring or even denying our inadequacies and displaying our strong points. We fear failure and go to ridiculous extremes in concealing our shortcomings. "I hope they see my grades," or "I'll impress them with my quick wit!" are typical attitudes.

Here we have a high risk for developing an inflated sense of our worthiness. We devote all our energy to hiding our midgets and displaying our giants. We must look perfect at all costs and become supersensitive to criticism. We rush to plug up every crack in our concealment, lest a trickle of criticism becomes a flood of truth about ourselves that shatters the fragile wall of self-confidence we have built.

The other type of phony façade is one in which we exaggerate our midgets. We become totally preoccupied with our inadequacies and spend all our energy trying to change them. We hate ourselves for what we are and soon come to hate everyone else also. Becoming far too self-critical and self-rejecting, we almost welcome failure, as we can use it as self-punishment. We lack sufficient confidence to make progress in our work and become paranoid about how we are perceived. We would rather stay away from people than risk displaying our midgets. Feeling that we have nothing of any worth to offer people, we never risk new friendships or new endeavors.

Both these phony façades place us in a perpetual bind, because we get reactions from others not to our true selves but to our façades. However, by some mental juggling we actually *expect* people to respond to our true selves. So, whenever we get a compliment or word of approval, it counts for little—since we never know whether it is our masks that are succeeding or our true selves. Conversely, whenever we are criticized, it hurts more than it should and is seldom constructive. This confusion places us in a bind, and we can never grow under these conditions. The seeds of psychological growth (social interaction with others) fall on the stony ground of our confusion and disbelief, preventing us from developing a realistic image of our true selves. To have a realistic self-image we must be open to honest feedback from those we can trust. Without this feedback our self-image remains a distortion, and our self-esteem continues as self-hate.

The causes of low self-esteem. Psychological theories differ greatly in the centrality which they give to the problem of low self-esteem and its causes. There are only two points of agreement I can identify within the major systems of psychology: (1) the foundations for self-esteem are laid early in life; and (2) interpersonal relationships play a major role in its development.

The main causes of low self-esteem are found in our early childhood and arise largely from how we relate to significant people in our lives, especially the members of our family. This places a tremendous responsibility on those of us who are parents. Unfortunately, if either or both parents suffer from a problem of low self-esteem, this problem can easily be perpetuated in their children. Many psychological studies support the commonly held view that positive and loving acceptance of the child by his parents is correlated with high self-esteem. However, if a parent is not self-accepting, it will be difficult for that parent to be accepting of a child.

Such parents will try to live out their unfulfilled ambitions through their children and will consequently make excessive demands of them. If a child fails, a parent may become critical and condemn the child. This condemnation then builds a feeling of inadequacy and unworthiness.

The most powerful force we have for controlling our children is our love. When our children are very small, we love them unconditionally. They may inconvenience or even irritate us, but we go on loving them anyway. As they get older we begin to punish them by withdrawing our love whenever they displease us, so that our love gradually becomes conditional. Not only do we reject when we withdraw our love, but we may even verbalize our rejection and use labels like "dumb" or "stupid." Whatever the parents do or say, the child slowly begins to internalize the rejections and starts labeling himself as "good" or "bad." The effect of this is devastating, especially during the critical years of early childhood.

There is overwhelming research evidence to show that a high level of self-esteem in the parents produces a more consistent atmosphere of unconditional love and acceptance, and this optimizes the development of high self-esteem in the children. Low self-esteem in the parents, even when it is hidden behind a superspiritual mask and covered by lots of church activity, seldom begets high self-esteem.

Closely related to the parents' self-esteem and related treatment of their children as a cause of low self-esteem are the values and expectations which parents unwittingly impose on their children. Certain societal values are more highly prized by some parents than others and may cause children to set up an internal system of self-rejection and self-punishment.

For example, our society highly prizes physical appearance. Through the medium of television and movies, we portray the type of physique and facial features equated with beauty or handsomeness and, in so doing, communicate to our children that unless they match these standards they will never make it. As the father of three daughters I know at first hand the pain of watching a child come to terms with his or her physique. Nearly every adolescent I have ever had in therapy has had some problem with physical appearance as a major concern about their self-esteem. As babies they were admired and adored. In the early years of life they were repeatedly told that they were "beautiful." Then one day, to their amazement, they realized that they were not perfectly beautiful. Being either too fat or too thin, too tall or too short, the sudden (or gradual) realization that their imperfections were many—and far removed from the ideals portrayed in the media—came as a bitter disappointment. The saddest aspect of this is that these values are very culturally dependent. The same physique in another culture might be more highly prized; but if you are unfortunate enough to have the "wrong" shape, size, and physical stature for your culture, you are doomed to self-rejection. There is nothing you can do about your midget, or so it seems.

As parents we buy into this system of values in many subtle ways, without giving it any thought. We send our children to have braces put on their teeth. We might even send them for some plastic surgery. What are we saying to them? "Appearance is important. You are not going to make it otherwise."

I am not advocating that we should not do what we can to improve our imperfections. I also go to the dentist and try to choose my clothing so as to do justice to my physique. But where do we draw the line? Eventually we will find imperfections which we cannot correct, and there is only one thing we can do then— find the freedom of self-acceptance.

But our society does not prize only appearance. Since it also prizes performance, those who feel inadequate in appearance can always try to make it with either intellectual achievement or success in some special endeavor. Get straight A's if you can—no matter what you look like! Excel in sports or bust! We start pushing our children from an early age. Perform, perform, perform! Of course, if you have both appearance and performance, you are a hero and will be worshiped. But since we cannot all succeed in compensating for nature's oversights, some of us must fail to make it and will end up feeling badly about ourselves and believing that we are of no value to anybody.

Christian Approaches to Self-Esteem

A common approach in Christian psychological articles about the problem of self-esteem is to find in God's love and acceptance of us the underlying dynamic for correcting low self-esteem. To experience unconditional love from God through His grace is to experience the basis for a healthy self-concept. This idea is unique to Christianity. There is nothing you *do* to earn favor with God. "God loves me just as I am; who am I not to love me?" is a common expression, and no doubt the acceptance of this idea at a very deep level can transform a person's life and give a sense of being valued by somebody—just as the midget did in the story at the beginning of this chapter. You cannot remain unmoved if you really believe the truth that God loves you unconditionally. It must bring a revolutionary change to your life, particularly with regard to your self-esteem. Then why do we find so many Christians with low self-esteem? I believe it is because this deals with only part of the problem.

For the midget in the bank, it was a revolutionary experience to find in God the first unconditional love and acceptance she had ever experienced. She had been valued, and now she could begin to value herself. The problem is that this experience of being greatly valued by God comes at a stage in most of our lives when it is difficult for it always to have a radical effect on the deeper problems of low self-esteem. The damage was done and the foundation laid for self-distortion and self-rejection at such an early age that it may take some time and a process of assimilation to reverse these effects. This is not to say that the Spirit of God cannot eradicate these roots and correct the faulty foundations of self-hate. I have personally witnessed many such apparently miraculous transformations. More commonly, however, these transformations take place as a slower process of growth, due to the inadequacy of our ability to really believe God and utilize His provisions. Unfortunately, many new Christians have been subjected to too much conflict, since they have been led to believe that everything is cured instantly. I am sure that every Christian psychotherapist is confronted by many such disillusioned and disappointed people who cannot understand why all their problems are still with them. While some aspects of Christian development may take place instantly, much is the result of process and growth. Especially in the area of self-hate, God must work retroactively as well as proactively, and this requires a constant attitude of commitment and willingness to change on our part.

To successfully deal with low self-esteem (as with many other problems in the area of emotion), it is necessary to reconstruct some aspects of your life, especially in the area of your thoughts and self-talk. Those of you who have lived the Christian life for many years will know that, while some steps seem to be revolutionary and instantaneous, most of the process is just plain hard work. The New Testament does not lead us to believe that from the moment of our commitment to God we will no longer have any problems or any need to repair past damage and inadequacies. "Think your way through," Paul says, "to a sober estimate of yourself" (*see* Romans 12:3). This means work.

We need to do an effective job of reconstruction of our self-attitude. For some of us, Christian commitment may mean an even greater risk of perpetuating low self-esteem, as we can easily set ourselves up to fear and avoid failure. We may set our ideals too high and develop a heightened awareness of our sinfulness and of our moral obligations. Every personal failure could then be exaggerated because it involves our life with God. We may easily increase our self-hate and self-rejection if we are not on guard.

So the problem of low self-esteem for the Christian is much more complex than many would have us believe—with roots that lie deep in the past and with the potential for becoming intensified by faulty ideas of failure. While the experience of God's love and acceptance is a necessary first step towards healing, it is *only* a first step, as we will see in the next section.

Calling Out Your Midgets

Let us now look more closely at Paul's prescription for repairing a distorted self-image as presented in Romans 12:1–3 (NEB). In my opinion, there are three important steps required for developing a healthy self-image from which self-esteem and not self-hate will emerge. These are consistent with a Christian view of personhood. The steps are: (1) the acceptance of God's unconditional love; (2) the development of realistic self-knowledge; and (3) complete self-acceptance.

1. God's unconditional love and acceptance in Christ. As I have already indicated, the first of these steps is foundational. Any effort to establish a sense of self-worth from within one's own being is a lost cause. By far the majority of us are doomed to failure by our appearance, our conversation, our behavior, and our lack of achievements, if we are expected to rely on our own resources. At best, each of us can erect a very flimsy façade and a phony self-image. Our basic worth must be founded outside of our human potential (or lack of it), and God in His redemptive work on the Cross and His subsequent call to all men to receive His salvation provides the essential basis for our worth. Becoming a "new creation" in Christ and finding that we are acceptable to God Himself *must* revolutionize our view of ourselves. Then we can have the courage and power to call out and deal with our midgets. No longer need we fear the ultimate of all rejections.

2. The development of realistic self-knowledge. Paul very clearly outlines this step: "Think your way to a sober estimate" (*see* Romans 12:3 NEB). Realistic self-knowledge must be an essential part of a healthy self-esteem. Any distortion of your self-understanding will produce a distorted self-image. If acceptance of yourself as a worthwhile being is based merely on the effective concealment and avoidance of your midgets (so that you are no longer aware of them), I do not believe you have a healthy self-esteem. Every time a midget raises his head you are going to be threatened. You must develop a realistic awareness of who and what you are, and this is where pride differs from high self-esteem. Many Christians fear that if they feel good about themselves they may be committing the sin of pride. But pride is characterized by *unrealistic* self-knowledge. It is self-concealment, not self-knowledge. The form of pride associated with an inflated self-image is usually a mechanism of defense which we have erected against feelings of inferiority. We may take "pride" in our accomplishments when we feel insecure and do not have a realistic understanding of our true strengths.

Pride is merely an exaggeration of our few giants in order to overcome the threat of our midgets. It is quite different from a healthy self-esteem, because the latter is based on *realistic* self-knowledge. Humility is the opposite of pride; it is not necessarily low self-esteem.

The development of realistic self-knowledge in a person with low self-esteem invariably requires that many distortions be corrected. It is common to find persons whose image of themselves comes from an earlier part of their lives and bears no relation to who they are now. Mostly we are not as bad as we have come to believe we are. Our midgets are *not* as small and as many as we fear, and over the years we have probably concealed or deliberately ignored our giants. Generally, we tend to exaggerate our failings and minimize our strengths.

It can be a most rewarding experience to take someone through the process of realistically evaluating these distortions and correcting them—to watch someone discover his true self. It can be the most rewarding of all the therapeutic tasks. But it is not necessary for everyone to solve this problem only in therapy. You can do it for yourself with the help of a close friend.

To facilitate this task, the process should be shared with someone else. While I know of those who have, in the privacy of prayer life, been able to successfully perform this task, God has created us to be in a fellowship relationship with others. Therefore, a close friend (or a small group) who can be trusted can help considerably. Begin by listing all the midgets you can identify, and alongside set down your giants. Then go over these with a close friend, carefully evaluating each one and adding or subtracting to the list according to your friend's advice. Do not try either to minimize or deny what you don't like or to resist your strengths. Your goal is to develop realistic knowledge and a clear description of yourself. Be honest. Have the courage to face your imperfections. Ask your friend to be genuine and yet not deliberately critical. Take it slowly and don't rush the process. In return you can do the same for your friend—in fact, it would be more effective if it were a mutually shared process. Having prepared this list of strengths and weaknesses and having obtained agreement on it from your friend, examine each of your midgets first. Ask yourself, "Are they really midgets at all?" Perhaps they are only "children"—aspects of your personality that have never been allowed to grow and develop—and with some effort and encouragement you might be able to transform them from liabilities to assets. We all have such underdeveloped areas in our lives. We can love better. We can be more transparent with others. We can be more dependable. Plan a way for turning these children into full-grown people. Often all it takes is a change in the way you view these liabilities. Believing that they can be improved is enough to begin the improvement.

You should also take a hard look at your giants. Perhaps you have never allowed yourself to indulge them. Talents are to be developed and used and not hidden away. In some strange manner, whenever there are too many midgets around, our giants tend to lose their power and go into hiding. A right attitude toward your strong points should help you develop more courage. Ask God to show you how you can use your strengths and dedicate them to Him.

Remember that this process is a dynamic one; you should not expect it to be completed at any one sitting. When you first start, you may find yourself dealing only with the very obvious and superficial aspects of your personality. As you work through these, you will find yourself discovering more subtle and elusive midgets and identifying giants you did not know existed. Keep it up and periodically repeat the process at various stages in your life. You will always find something new to work on.

3. Complete self-acceptance. The third step, complete self-acceptance, is the most difficult, mainly because it involves dealing with much irrationality in your thoughts and beliefs. You may find it easy to identify your obvious strengths and weaknesses, especially if you have the help of an insightful and honest friend. But the step of complete self-acceptance can only be taken by yourself.

Why is this step necessary? Thinking one's way through to "a sober estimate" involves more than just giving intellectual assent to a set of positive and negative qualities about yourself. There may be some midgets you will be able to change if you are sufficiently motivated and know how to use the resources of your faith. These changes can be accomplished (or at least the process commenced) without much difficulty. But what are you going to do about the midgets you cannot change? Become despairing? Continue your self-hate? This will only cause you to become more resentful, and the more you know about yourself the greater will be your resentfulness. Whether it is something you are dissatisfied with and can change—or whether it is something that is fixed and unchangeable—you must begin at the same point: *complete self-acceptance.*

In asking you to take this step, I am not advocating that you be resigned to your inadequacies, that you give up seeking a way to change. This is simply a step in which you realistically recognize where you are *now*. It frees you from the shackles of self-condemnation and avoids the trap of not knowing what to do with what you can't change. You must move yourself to the place of accepting without resentfulness what you cannot change, and knowing where you stand on those aspects that can be changed. This takes courage. And this is where Christ can make the difference in your life. It is on the basis of what He has done for you that you can accept yourself just as you are.

A friend of mine taught me this lesson so forcibly about fifteen years ago that I have never forgotten it. He was a graduate of Fuller Seminary and had gone to Africa to do mission work. He was a charming man, loved by everyone who met him. But he hadn't always been this way. In his earlier life he had been overcome by one midget: *He hated his nose*. He saw it as long and protruding and so despised it that he began to despise his whole being. One day, by himself, he came to terms with his midget. He had realistic self-knowledge—it stared at him out of the mirror every day—but he had never taken the step of total self-acceptance. On his knees before God, he prayed a prayer of self-acceptance—and a fantastic sense of freedom followed as he set himself free from his midget. From that day on he was a different man. "Here, world, you better take me as I am, because that's all I've got!" was his new attitude, and this freedom made him beautiful to everyone who met him. No one even noticed his nose! He had the courage to accept himself unconditionally and set himself free.

But this step must also include making room for failure. We fear failure more than we care to admit, and since we are only human it is inevitable that failure will be our experience regularly. Your development of realistic self-knowledge should therefore include an honest appraisal of your failure proneness and your attitude to failure. Self-acceptance must then include some permission for yourself to fail, so that failure will not devastate your self-image.

All of this can be obstructed by irrational mental processes. We have a tremendous capacity for irrational thinking. Feelings of inadequacy and inferiority can often be based on unrealistic expectations for oneself—which in turn can lead to irrational beliefs of low self-worth. For example, the unrealistic expectation that one must succeed—*at all times* in *everything*—is a common one. Ridiculous? Of course it is, when stated as bluntly as this. But most of us behave as if it were absolutely true. Check yourself out the next time you fail at something. How much allowance do you make for failing? If you fail once in one hundred times, do you give yourself a high score or a low score? No matter how many times you have succeeded, my guess is that the moment you fail you will come down hard on yourself.

Failures are to grow by. Then why do we use them for self-destruction? God does not demand that we succeed at everything we do. In any event, most of our failures are of our own creation. We prepare ourselves for failure by setting unrealistic goals and then expecting that we must meet them without any provision for a miss.

I know a housewife, for example, who is criticized by her husband every time the meal she has cooked is not perfect. Does she stop and evaluate the fact that she may have cooked it perfectly nine times in a row and this is the first failure out of ten attempts? No, she is devastated over one criticism. Instead of saying to herself, "It is unfortunate that I can succeed only nine times out of ten," she says, "I have failed—I am a bad cook." She may not be able to do anything about her husband's criticism, but she can do a lot about her reaction!

Unrealistic expectations and beliefs like these need to be challenged constantly if you are going to eradicate your self-hate. When stated in their extremes, their ridiculous nature becomes apparent. They are unfounded, have no evidence to substantiate them, and need to be discarded as quickly as possible if we are going to move ourselves to the place of realistic self-knowledge and complete self-acceptance. Our Christian Gospel is amazingly free of these irrational expectations. First, we are accepted for what we are. Provision is then made for dealing with our failures and inadequacies. We do not have to depend entirely on ourselves. In fact, we are not expected to, but have resources outside of ourselves to accomplish our "perfecting." The irrationality of a lot of what we see in our Christian communities is of our own creation. The Gospel is inherently "healthy" and should create in its followers those who are sound in mind as well as in spirit. If it fails to do this, the fault clearly lies with us.

Summary

Low self-esteem is caused by self-hate. Our culture sets us up to experience our inadequacies in such a way that we develop a distorted image of ourselves, more commonly feeling hopelessly inadequate rather than overconfident. While Paul's prescription in Romans 12:3 is addressed to the problem of conceit, the principles for remedying self-hate are the same:

- Accept God's unconditional love
- Develop realistic self-knowledge
- Accept yourself unconditionally

While the acceptance of God's unconditional love is foundational to a healthy self-esteem, active steps need to be taken to achieve a realistic self-image and total and unconditional self-acceptance. Irrational expectations and erroneous ideas about failure must be dealt with if a healthy self-esteem is to be maintained.

Additional Reading

1. *Self-Esteem*. Craig W. Ellison (Ed.). Oklahoma City: Southwestern Press.
2. *Psychology of Self-Esteem*. Nathaniel Branden. New York: Bantam.

3. *Hide or Seek*. James Dobson. Old Tappan, New Jersey:
   Fleming H. Revell.
4. *The Search for Self-Respect*. Maxwell Maltz. New York:
   Bantam.
5. Mark 12:28–34.
   Romans 12:1–5.

8

Freedom From Guilt

GUILT IS ALL AROUND US. We feel guilty about our children, our parents, our jobs, even our pets—just everything. It is hard to escape from it. Not all this guilt is neurotic or bad, as it serves to keep us fulfilling our obligations and acting as responsible members of society. Our credit system depends on it! We pay our debts because of guilt; we often love because of guilt; and—the saddest thing of all—sometimes we even love God only out of guilt!

Of all the emotions, guilt must be the one with the most overlap between psychology and theology. Theologians, philosophers, and psychologists have talked about guilt since the dawn of their respective disciplines, and all have tried to find in its understanding the key to spiritual, mental, and emotional health. Unfortunately, though, when theologians talk about guilt they often mean something quite different from what psychologists mean. This can be very confusing to the layperson, since what they mainly experience is the form of guilt which psychologists talk about. Theological guilt may never have been experienced, though it is nevertheless real.

The misunderstanding of the difference between that form of guilt which is entirely psychological and that which is theological causes considerable tension in sincere and well-meaning Christians. In their effort to be devout, they make themselves vulner-

133

able to increased psychological guilt. When this guilt is experienced, it is interpreted as spiritual rather than psychological—and they respond to it with feelings of self-condemnation which only create further guilt proneness. This cycle can sometimes produce a deep depression.

It is important, therefore, that we draw a clear distinction between psychological and spiritual guilt. Emotional and spiritual healthiness depends largely on how effectively we deal with both forms. The distinction between the two will become clear as we proceed. While much psychological guilt has no spiritual components, being the consequence of our early upbringing and training, I do believe that God has provided for dealing with both this form of guilt as well as that which is truly spiritual. The purpose of this chapter, however, will be to deal primarily with the important implications of our *psychological* guilt.

Christians Are Not Exempt From Guilt Problems

A young man once came to see me about a problem he considered to be serious. I was his last desperate hope! He had been counseled by many ministers and evangelists without any relief, and his problem only became worse. Four years previously he had made a Christian commitment by responding to an altar call at an evangelistic meeting. Thereafter he had made some progress in his faith and had now offered himself as a candidate for the Christian ministry. The problem as he described it was that, whenever he attended an evangelistic meeting and the altar call was given, he felt an overwhelming compulsion to respond to the invitation and go forward. He could not understand why he should feel this compulsion, as he was secure in his basic commitment. Needless to say, whenever he counseled with a minister he was told that he had to take the urge seriously, since it could be that God was speaking to him. He had become very despondent. He developed a fear of going to church and was becoming a recluse.

As we explored the problem together, it became obvious to me that the problem was one of psychological guilt. Early in his life, strong pressure from his parents to conform to their belief system had conditioned him to have a guilt response every time a call to repentance was made. After I explained the psychological mechanisms involved and expanded more fully for him on the real meaning of forgiveness, he slowly began to experience freedom from his emotional pain. His Christian commitment also began to take on new meaning.

Perhaps this may be an extreme example of the confusion that a misunderstanding of the various forms of guilt can cause in a sincerely devout person. To a lesser extent this misunderstanding can cause us just as much misery. The fact is, as Christian believers we are not exempt from the psychological mechanisms of neurotic guilt and—unless we learn how to tell one type from the other—will always be handicapped in our growth toward spiritual and psychological health. Not only are we exempt, but our belief system may in fact aggravate the problem. We can easily create for ourselves an environment that places unrealistically high demands on our standards of morality and our subtle conviction that we can never meet God's standard for purity. When coupled with perfectionistic traits and an inability to tolerate failure, these beliefs may create a form of neurotic guilt. This is of our own creating, and what lies behind it is a faulty understanding of the nature of grace and forgiveness.

Unresolved guilt.   I repeatedly encounter Christian believers who have not resolved their guilt proneness, or who have developed an exaggerated guilt mechanism, not all of which is spiritually healthy. Later in this chapter I will clarify the real nature of spiritual guilt, but at this point it is sufficient to emphasize that being a Christian does not automatically correct guilt problems.

It is true that spiritual guilt, when acknowledged, can cause a valid state of psychological guilt. However, this form of guilt does not have the same irrational quality that much neurotic guilt has. It is more constructive, reparative, and amenable to forgiveness than neurotic guilt.

For example, let us suppose that one has perfectionist tendencies. A perfectionist is someone who cannot avoid doing anything without making impossible, unrealistic demands on himself. Some of us have perfectionistic *traits,* in that we must tidy up

behind us because we cannot stand to see anything dirty or disor-
ganized. These traits are not necessarily unhealthy. The true perfectionist, however, has a built-in system of self-punishment
which is applied whenever he feels that he has not measured up to
the standards of performance set for himself. Such people may
feel that the right thing to do is to be out of bed by at least 6:00
A.M. If for some reason they oversleep, they will punish themselves by self-criticism or depression for the remainder of the day.
If, in addition, they believe that God wants them to be out of bed
by that early hour, they could easily interpret their guiltiness as
God's speaking to them. Such guiltiness does not easily respond to
forgiveness. It demands punishment as the only way to relief.

It is possible, of course, for ministers and evangelists unwittingly to utilize psychological mechanisms for creating a state of
guilt in their listeners. This misuse has long been the cause of
concern in Christian psychological circles, as it can give rise to
spurious conversions and commitments which, in turn, can
hamper further spiritual development in the individual concerned.

I have seen this abuse carried so far that it precipitated a series
of suicides in one Christian community, but that's another story.
Whether or not God can use such abuse is difficult for us to decide,
but in the long run this misuse does not produce meaningful
conversions. When God works in the life of an individual,
psychological tricks are unnecessary and may even be detrimental.

The central role of guilt in the neuroses.   Again and again
psychologists and psychiatrists have returned to placing guilt at
the heart of the neuroses. David Hume, the eighteenth-century
Scottish philosopher, claimed that guilt was fundamental to
every problem in human personality. Karen Horney contends
that guilt feelings play a central role in neurosis. By this she does
not mean that all neurotics are immoral, but merely that they
feel more guilty. No one has tried to understand the role of guilt
more than Sigmund Freud, the founder of psychoanalysis. He
strongly contended for the centrality of guilt. Rollo May, who
takes an existential approach, sees neurotic guilt as the end

product of unconfronted, unresolved, normal guilt. It is he who also claims that normal guilt is both necessary and healthy, an important point that is frequently overlooked. And so we could go on. There is hardly a prominent psychological theorist who has not given a seat of prominence to the problems of guilt.

For me, the most significant thing about guilt is the frequency with which it triggers other emotional reactions or is triggered by them. It is probably the most common chained emotion. We might get angry at our children and shout at them and then are almost immediately moved by a reaction of feeling guilty. We feel sorry for what we have done and then try to reduce our guilt. The net result of this is a large swing from shouting and anger to placating and reconciling—all very unsettling to our children.

Or we might become depressed by something. As soon as we are aware of our depression we feel guilty and react because of this guilt with a further sense of loss, thus deepening the depression.

Guilt and anger. Guilt can trigger anger very easily. I might come home from work, having forgotten to stop and buy something my wife has asked me to get. As I walk in the front door and see my wife, I remember what it was I should have purchased. I feel guilty, but rather than admit my guilt I react by getting angry: "You always ask me to get something for you when you know I am busy. You know I've got more important things to think about." By attacking her, I both alleviate my guilt feelings and at the same time prevent her from attacking me for my forgetfulness.

Many a wife has probably been trapped by that helpless look on her husband's face as he peers into his sock drawer and finds it empty. "You should have told me you were near the end of your socks," she protests in anger. "You knew very well that Mother was coming to visit and that I would not have time to do the wash on my usual day." Why the anger? Because she feels guilty. A little voice tells her that she could have prevented this by just a little forethought, but she didn't. She also knew that her mother was coming and could have planned accordingly, but she didn't—so she feels guilty and anger is triggered.

Where Does Guilt Proneness Come From?

The most common idea that laypersons have about where guilt comes from is that it is produced by something we call a "conscience." But what is the conscience? Does it exist in a special part of the brain? Are we born with it, or do we learn it? These questions are not as easy to answer as you might expect.

Philosophers have tended to see conscience as a form of moral consciousness—a sense of what is right or wrong—without being too concerned about where it comes from. Theologians have tended to emphasize that it is "the rule of divine power expressing itself in a person's judgments." Generally, psychologists see conscience as an expression of values that have been acquired from parents and teachers and become internalized as part of one's personality.

For our purpose we need not be too concerned about being technically correct. There may or may not be a "conscience center" in the brain. It is sufficient for us to recognize that we have a God-given capacity to evaluate the rightness or wrongness of our thoughts and actions and to feel good or bad about the outcome. Either feeling good or feeling bad is part of our conscience. Psychologists and theologians owe a great deal of gratitude to Freud, the founder of psychoanalysis, for emphasizing that much of this mechanism goes on without awareness and that there are two aspects to it. The ideal or positive aspect pushes us to strive for or be attracted to that which we see as good, and the prohibitive or negative aspect condemns us for what is bad. This latter aspect includes the many commands and prohibitions we have taken into our value system, mainly through the influence of our parents. The state of tension or self-condemnation we feel whenever we evaluate something as wrong is what we call "guilt."

How do we learn what to feel guilty about? Mainly from our parents, and most of it is learned very early in life. In a simplified way, the process is as follows: When we first enter the world we are loved unconditionally. Fortunately, we are loved for what we are, not for what we do. We are the pride and joy of our parents, and even though we may be an inconvenience and cause some extra work, we are generally appreciated and accepted. As we begin to grow, however, our parents begin to replace their uncon-

ditional love with love that is conditional. We are loved when we
do the right things, but not loved (and perhaps even rejected)
when we do wrong. The withdrawal of parental love partly occurs
because of the anger and frustration our parents experience at
our not doing those things they want us to. Slowly, as we continue
to grow, we begin to internalize the conflict between being accepted and being rejected and begin to condemn ourselves without
waiting for parental condemnation. There are, of course, other
factors which enter into the development of our guilt proneness,
but mainly it is a process of creating substitute parents within
ourselves. Sometimes our parents may even add a little flavor to
the process by throwing in a few words like "You are dumb, aren't
you?" or "You are stupid, bad, and disgusting!" and we may also
internalize these as a sense of shame. Needless to say, our self-
esteem will suffer as a by-product of this guilt induction, so that
guilt proneness and low self-esteem frequently occur together.

Surprisingly, physical disciplining, properly administered,
produces a much healthier internalized value system than do the
verbal methods most often employed by parents. The verbal
methods are used mainly because it is easier to shout across the
room to reprimand a child than it is to go to the child and deal
with the behavior. Physical disciplining does not necessarily have
to involve hitting or spanking. It can include a variety of techniques such as loss of privileges, time spent away from toys, the
TV, or friends. Moderate and appropriate physical punishment is
not as damaging as might be expected. It is less likely to lead to
guilt problems—because the penalty for the misdeed is paid immediately. It is over with. It doesn't become prolonged and require a "You are bad!" message; nor is there a forcing of the child
to apologize. Verbal methods, such as shouting or saying shame-
ful things in order to control behavior or punish misdeeds, can be
much more cruel than physical punishment. Think back to your
own childhood. The chances are that you remember the verbal
cruelties more easily than any physical punishment (provided the
latter was not excessively cruel itself).

Not only do we use our love and approval to train our children's
consciences, but we also use them to manipulate and to punish or
hurt back. We force our children to ask for forgiveness whenever

they have wronged us, or we create in them strong feelings of guilt because they don't love us enough or because they get angry at us for what we do to them. The effects of this manipulation are deeply embedded into the personality of the child and last throughout life, as many of you can no doubt attest. I know a seventy-year-old man who still responds to situations just as if his mother were still hovering over him!

Two Types of Conscience

Can you let your conscience be your guide? Not always. You may be on shaky ground whenever you use your conscience to help you make a decision or guide your behavior. Conscience is usually helpful, but—since it can be so easily distorted and is merely the reflection of an internalized overstrict parent—we need to be cautious.

Conscience can also be warped in another direction. It can be underdeveloped and inadequate to guide us because it lacks any sensitivity. When someone is brought up in an atmosphere of neglect, there is invariably no parent to internalize.

Conscience can be a problem in both extremes. On the one hand it may be overdeveloped and dominate our personality, causing us to make extreme demands on ourselves. We then respond to irrational ideas as to what is the right behavior for a given situation. We impose moral standards on ourselves more out of the fear of the consequences than because of any genuine concern for morality and tend to feel guilty almost all the time about everything we do. It becomes impossible to assert ourselves and stand up for very basic rights without feeling guilty, since we cannot say no to a request and have great difficulty confronting someone who is hurting us. These are the sorts of problems which develop when our conscience dominates us.

On the other hand, it is possible to suffer from an inadequately developed conscience. In this case we experience very little anxiety when we cause pain to others. It is possible to engage in behaviors that most people consider to be immoral and yet feel no tension. While we may conform to the standards of behavior of those around us, we do so in order to "keep the peace" or be accepted, rather than out of a sense of what we believe to be right or wrong. It becomes commonplace to make the same mistake over and over again and not benefit from the experience. We seldom really feel sorry for what we do and resent any effort anyone may make to punish us. In its extreme form this lack of conscience is called a "conduct disorder," as it frequently causes the person to be in trouble with authority figures or the law.

A normal conscience.   Obviously, somewhere between these two extremes there is a region that we can describe as normal. A normal conscience exists when there is enough concern about the welfare of others that a tension is created whenever their rights are infringed. Such concern is not dominated by an exaggerated feeling of worthlessness about oneself, nor are the basic beliefs that underly the conscience totally unfounded or irrational. The person with a normal conscience understands why something is right or wrong and does not experience condemnation of himself without an adequate basis in reality. For instance, one who *accidentally* fails to stop at a traffic signal—and then continues to feel depressed throughout the remainder of the day because of guilt— is failing to make some allowance for human imperfection. The person who *deliberately* drives through a traffic signal because he is in a hurry deserves to feel guilty afterwards. However, if the resulting guilt feeling is unduly prolonged, even this latter person may lack the capacity to forgive himself and to benefit from such an experience by making sure that he does not do it again.

In summary, therefore, I would say that a normal, healthy, and well-balanced conscience has the following qualities:

1. A normal conscience is concerned with "morality" (the correct source of moral attitudes) and not with "moralism" (the preoccupation with right behaviors). Moralism is more concerned about the appearance of the behavior than with the reason for it. What our parents teach us is usually mere moralism. Their underlying message is: "Do it this way and you will please me." Later in life we still do things just to please our internalized parent without knowing *why* we do it. When the behavior is wrong, therefore, we feel guilty—even if a truly moral principle has not been violated. True morality, on the other hand, knows why something is wrong. Because it endangers the lives of others,

it is bad to go through a red traffic light without stopping. Throwing off the moralisms of our upbringing and developing a well-balanced morality are necessary steps toward developing the freedom to experience our emotions in a healthy way.

As Christians, it is very easy to become engrossed in moralisms. We can become preoccupied with behaving the "right" way, with no understanding of the underlying moral issues. By contrast, the Gospel is more concerned with morality than with moralism. Righteousness has to do with the *source* of right behavior. If the source is moral, the behavior will be righteous. If the source is not moral, no matter how perfect is our behavior by outward standards, it will not be righteous.

2. A healthy conscience should be flexible not rigid, and it should be sensitive yet sensible. It should alert us to wrong just as pain alerts us to disease, but it should not proceed to punish us unnecessarily for what we have done. A well-balanced conscience should allow us to weigh all the factors involved in the wrongdoing, so that we can have an honest understanding of the limits of our responsibility. Could we have avoided what happened? Were there factors beyond our control? Was it really our fault? Can we easily rectify the wrong? A healthy conscience permits us to ask this sort of question. An overbearing conscience condemns us without mercy and will allow no mitigating factors. This should not be confused with a tendency to make excuses for what we have done wrong. These excuses are often dishonest and are designed to buy off our conscience with deception. If we are really guilty, we should feel guilty. What we then do with the guilt is the most important question.

3. A well-balanced conscience does not engage in excessive self-blaming, self-condemnation, or self-punishment. If we allow our conscience to do this, we only destroy the learning value of the failure experience. "Failures are to grow by," but we keep wanting to use them to punish ourselves—and this is self-obstructive. If we hurt someone with sharp words, we should learn from the experience not to do it again. If we have fallen prey to some immoral behavior, we should also learn from that experience. Guilt should serve as a warning sign that something is wrong—not as a self-punishment device. If we become preoccupied with

self-blame and self-punishment, we will not be able to utilize the failure as a learning experience.

4. A normal conscience knows how to obtain and accept forgiveness, whether this forgiveness is from other people or from God. In fact, we cannot stop self-punishment until we know how to obtain forgiveness. We must learn to trade our self-punishment for God's forgiveness. If someone we have harmed will not forgive us, we then receive that forgiveness from God. We must not let our failures continue to cast a dark shadow of guilt across our freedom and happiness, since we can receive the ultimate in all forgiveness. To punish oneself is to make a mockery of the Cross. Christ wanted to carry responsibility for all our failures, so why not let Him do His work completely?

Neurotic guilt.   While it takes an overdeveloped conscience to create neurotic guilt, not everyone with a supersensitive conscience is neurotic. The difference between having a demanding conscience and having guilt which is neurotic is in the *degree* and *quality* of the guilt. Your guilt can be labeled as "neurotic" when it has the following qualities:

- You have a strong sense of your own evil.
- You feel guilty nearly all the time without adequate justification.
- You keep labeling yourself as "bad."
- Your guilt reactions last a long time.
- Your guilt is triggered by imagined wrongs, and then you cannot stop the guilt.
- Your guilt reactions to little wrongs are extreme.
- Your guilt so incapacitates you that you cannot relate to anyone and want to be alone.
- Your guilt causes you to want to take extreme actions (such as suicide) to remedy your wrongs.
- You cannot stop remembering all your past misdeeds.

Let me illustrate some of these. You may get angry and shout at your son before he leaves for school. Yet, as soon as he is gone, you experience great discomfort because of your guilt, and it lasts throughout the day. You can't wait until you can do something to alleviate your guilt. When your son comes home you find some way to please him and thus compensate for your shouting. If this happened repeatedly, it would be neurotic. First, you are not attempting to deal with the cause of your anger (perhaps some disciplining would rectify your son's behavior), and second, you are teaching your son how he can manipulate you with guilt. In any event, guilt should be resolved with a simple apology and not with an elaborate ritual of compensation for the harm done.

Let's say that we have accidentally tramped on an insect and killed it. Suddenly we are overcome with a terrible feeling of guilt. "How could I do such a thing? Insects have a right to live as much as people! Couldn't I have looked where I was walking?" This sort of guilt (which is not uncommon) is clearly neurotic. While it doesn't always take the form of insect killing, the same principles apply when we bump other people's automobiles or when we must put an aged and sickly dog to sleep. We say to ourselves, "Could I not have avoided that?" We make no allowance for accidents, and even if we do respect insect life, we cannot walk through a garden while examining every area of footpath to make sure it is free of insects. Neurotic guilt is therefore frequently characterized by no actual violation—or the violation is of petty, internalized, irrational principles. It can have a powerful negative effect on us, removing our freedom and robbing us of happiness.

Neurotic guilt can even be caused by imagined violations. I know someone who often fantasizes that he is punishing those who have harmed him. When he is finished mutilating them, an intense guilt overtakes him. Despite the fact that no actual harm has been caused to anyone, he responds with guilt more appropriate to real harm. Naturally, his problem is much more serious than the disturbed guilt mechanism.

While many of my readers will not experience guilt to this extreme, there may be more subtle traps of neurotic quality that imprison them. Perhaps you recognize one of the following self-talk statements: "I *must* do this," "I *should* do that," or "I've just *got to!*" It's just possible that you are being controlled and manipulated by what you think others will say, or you have an exaggerated fear that you will not please everybody. Whenever you break one of these rules, you feel terrible and engage in self-condemnation. While some "shoulds" in life are necessary, they are mainly arbitrary and irrational and need careful evaluation before you respond to them. Strangely, when they are legitimate, they never feel like "shoulds." I should support and care for my family—but I hardly ever feel it is a "should." I'm only too glad to do it. The irrational "shoulds" we lay on ourselves make prisons for us without our realizing it. Fortunately, we hold the key to unlocking this prison and can, with careful thought and attention to the principles I am enunciating here, free ourselves from neurotic guilt. If we can't, professional help should be sought from someone we feel we can trust.

Some Important Determiners of Guilt

Developing and maintaining a healthy conscience and appropriate guilt response are not things that happen automatically. These attitudes require constant cultivation. You can pass through your childhood unscathed and then find that you fall prey in early adulthood (or any later stage of your life, for that matter) to influences that increase your guilt proneness.

In Christian circles there are three important determiners of an aggravated conscience. These are:

1. An inadequate God concept
2. An inadequate sin concept
3. An inadequate forgiveness concept

Anyone reared in an environment where these inadequate concepts are propagated will find himself prone to guilt problems in later life. The influence of belief systems erected around these inadequacies can be great enough to affect someone even in later life.

I was introduced to such a system shortly after my conversion at age eighteen and was subjected to many erroneous ideas related to these concepts. As a result I experienced a marked increase in my guilt proneness which lasted for nearly five years, before I became aware of what was happening. Rather than finding my early Christian experience to be happy and fulfilling, it became burdensome and depressing. Looking back now, I regret that there wasn't someone to correct my erroneous ideas. At least two of my close friends who were converted at the same time fell victim to these erroneous ideas and were so depressed by the experience that they gave up their commitments. As far as I know, they have not returned to the Christian faith since then.

1. An inadequate God concept.   We hardly ever pause to reflect on the concept of God which we have constructed in our minds. We assume that everyone else has the same idea about who God is. I have researched the variability of concepts of God among different Christian groups for some years now, and this has confirmed my contention that Christians show marked differences in their understanding of the nature of God. I have examined the concept of God as seen by missionary groups, ministers, and lay people of various denominations and found that people, even within the same church group, have markedly different ideas. Women have a different concept from men. Marked differences are found with age, and, of course, different cultures produce quite different ideas about the nature of God. The net result is that we all end up in adult life seeing God slightly differently. This difference is not always important, but there are some extreme ideas which can influence our emotional health.

Your God Is Too Small by J. B. Phillips is a most important book on this topic. The author warns us to be careful about the image that we form of God. If our understanding of God is that He is nothing more than a form of policeman, or if God is seen as harsh and punitive, we may experience considerable guilt proneness. As I have worked in therapy with people who have developed an inadequate God concept, it has become obvious that they have frequently merely internalized images of their parents, usually the father. If he has been harsh and punitive, they tend to see God this way.

2. An inadequate sin concept.   Guilt problems can also arise when we do not have a clear understanding of the nature of sin. Our conscience can bother us even when no sin has been committed. We feel guilty about so many things, and few of them can be classified as sin. Frequently, guilt over social rules and mores is only relevant to one culture and not another, yet we label breaking these rules as "sin." We can easily make our consciences into a god. I am familiar with the customs of some of the tribes of southern Africa and know how new missionaries, beginning work among these tribes, have great difficulty at first in adapting to the different sin concept of these people. They cannot understand why a primitive man who is an avowed Christian would take food belonging to the missionary and not see it as stealing. In actual fact, something like food is viewed as common property, and these tribes do not recognize food as belonging to anyone. Food is communal property and can be taken at will by anyone in need of it. The western missionary's law is confusing to them, because their assumptions are so completely different.

But we can develop just as erroneous an idea about what sin is because our assumptions are not correct. I doubt whether everything we label "sin" is actually sin in God's eyes. On the other hand, there may be many sinful things which we do not recognize as sin. Prominent psychologist Karl Menninger recently wrote a book called *Whatever Became of Sin?* In it he asks why we have dropped this concept from our psychological vocabulary. In our eagerness to resolve our guilt problems, we run the danger of creating an inadequate sin concept—but in the other direction.

3. An inadequate forgiveness concept. Forgiveness is the genius of Christianity. No other religious belief system places it as central as the Gospel does. What else is the Cross about? God knew when He created us that we would need forgiveness. It is for *our* benefit. I have a sneaking suspicion that most Christians have the irrational idea lurking in the back of their minds that perhaps God needs to forgive us more than we need His forgiveness. It's true that He *wants* to forgive us more than we are willing to receive it, but does He *need* to give us forgiveness? When we have sinned or our conscience is bothering us, we believe that somehow He needs us to ask for forgiveness, as if He benefited in some way from it. No, it's the other way around. God has provided forgiveness because *we* need it. This is the only way we can deal with our consciences, whether they are healthy or not.

Leslie Weatherhead has said, "The forgiveness of God is the most powerful therapeutic idea in the world. If a person can really believe that God has forgiven him, he can be saved from neuroticism."

Summary

Despite the centrality given to forgiveness in the Christian Gospel, guilt problems are prevalent among Christian people. While the foundation for guilt problems is laid in early childhood, it is possible to develop an excessive guilt responsiveness later in life. An abnormally sensitive conscience can give rise to guilt feelings which (1) do not respond to forgiveness (whether from people or God); (2) do not motivate people to make constructive amends; and (3) are the product of moralism (concern for surface behavior) and not morality. Neurotic guilt tends to be vague and pervasive. It responds to the slightest provocation, often becoming preoccupied with self-condemnation and self-punishment.

To develop a healthy guilt response, one must challenge one's irrational internalized parents, thus developing a more rational and flexible conscience, a right attitude to failure, and the courage to take responsibility for mistakes without engaging in self-punishment.

For emotional freedom from neurotic guilt it is essential to have *a proper God concept,* where God is not seen just as a policeman waiting to punish; *a proper sin concept,* where one's conscience does not become a god and where one's understanding of sin is properly informed by the truth of Scripture; and *a proper forgiveness concept,* where the true meaning of what God has provided is fully understood.

Additional Reading

1. *Your God Is Too Small.* J. B. Phillips. New York: Macmillan.
2. *Guilt-Free.* Dick and Paula McDonald. New York: Grosset & Dunlap.
3. *Release From Fear and Anxiety.* Cecil Osborne. Waco, Texas: Word.

4. *The Guilt Trip.* Hal Lindsey. Grand Rapids, Michigan: Zondervan.
5. *Guilt and Grace.* Paul Tournier. New York: Harper & Row.
6. Romans 5.

9
Freedom to Love

A POPULAR SONG of recent years has words that go like this: "Loving you is easy, 'cause you're beautiful . . . ." It is set to one of those melodies which will haunt you all day long. Even now, as I am reminded of it, it has hooked me again, and it will be tomorrow before I will have set it aside. It is a beautiful song. But what an indictment against our society! *It's easy to love you–because you're beautiful.*

I am not disagreeing with the lyricist. In fact, I'm in full agreement. These words are absolutely *true*, and that's the tragedy. The lyricist is just telling it as it is.

What's my gripe? Simply this: What if you're not beautiful? What if you cannot attract attention either to your physique or to your psyche? What if you have little to offer in return, if you're just a nonentity as so many feel they are? Can you then expect to be loved? Do you have the prospect of lots of attention, as people fall over themselves to get to know you? I doubt it. If I were to judge by the desperate hunger of the many who have passed through my office, I would have to conclude that we are a love-starved society, and this starvation is due primarily to two factors: (1) we don't know what love is; and (2) we don't know how to love.

The result is that we can only love when it's easy and when there's a payoff for ourselves. We can love when the object we love is beautiful. This makes it both easy and profitable. We can love when we get something in return. "Be nice and loving to my

150

mother. You know she's left us something in her will!" is so characteristic of our age that we hardly ever notice our ulterior motives anymore.

The Importance of Relationships

We cannot consider love without thinking of people and relationships. There are those, of course, who have become so disillusioned about finding love in human beings that they have invested all their love in pets. Animals can provide us with a rich source of unconditional acceptance which is necessary for the satisfaction of our love needs. But we cannot isolate ourselves from people without paying for it in distorted personalities and disturbed priorities.

The most important thing we do as social creatures is *relate*. It may be difficult and cause us much psychological pain, but relate we must—and with other *people*.

Most of what I have discussed in this book so far is the consequence of relationships. Our emotions never take place outside of the realm of people. Seldom are emotional problems not relationship oriented—and relationship is what love is all about. Until you know what love really is—how to love and how to receive love—you are an incomplete person. You will never be fulfilled nor deeply satisfied until you are free to love.

True, human relationships can be the source of the most intense misery the human frame is capable of, and many people are unhappy and lonely because they cannot establish and sustain adequate social relationships. Most suicides, for instance, are over broken or unsatisfactory relationships, as are most divorces. But whatever way you look at it, these problems finally boil down to problems of neither knowing what love is nor how to love. When we are able to love, human relationships become the source of such deep satisfactions and lasting happiness that there is nothing else to compare with it. Kings have even given up their thrones for love.

Love—Christian-Style

There are many things you can do in isolation—but being a Christian is not one of them. If you hate people, better not expect to be a Christian. Actually, that's not quite true. If you hate people, the *only* way to go is to become a Christian. You will then find a way to love them.

I am utterly convinced that the New Testament's emphasis on love is intentional. In contrast to the Old Testament, love permeates every page of the New. Every Gospel and every Epistle has something to say about love—and for good reason! Why? I think for two reasons:

1. God knows us.   He knows we are primarily social creatures and He knows what we need. Our deepest needs will be satisfied only if we follow His prescription.

2. The Gospel has no meaning and no relevance outside the context of relationships.   It is here that we glorify God. It is here that His purpose is fulfilled. God demands that we love one another—it is not optional. "He that loveth not knoweth not God . . ." (1 John 4:8 KJV). "If a man say, I love God, and hateth his brother, he is a liar . . ." (1 John 4:20 KJV).

Thus, both because God knows us and because His Gospel depends on it, we are obligated to come to terms with love. But don't make the mistake of thinking that because you are a Christian you know everything there is to know about love. True, you've been exposed to the ultimate demonstration of love, but implementing it in your life—to your neighbor, friend, husband, wife, and children—is another story. If you're having problems here, take heart. So do all of us. With a better understanding of what love is, you should be able to overcome your major obstacles.

Misconceptions About Love

No psychologist nor philosopher has thus far been able to define love adequately and to everyone's satisfaction. Though difficult to describe, all of us have experienced it enough to be able to recognize what it is.

The problem of defining love arises because of its complexity. There are many kinds of love and many ways of giving and receiving love. We will not be concerned here with the romantic or sexual aspects of love, legitimate as these may be. They fulfill very real and deep needs in all of us and cannot be lightly discarded. Even they, however, depend for their satisfaction on a much deeper and more lasting emotion we could call "true love." The Greeks had different words for the different types of love, but I prefer not to separate them, as it is my strong conviction that all forms of love have a common thread around which the others are woven to make a particular pattern of love. The romantic and the sexual threads do not have to be present in true love. Frequently they only confuse the picture and make it more difficult to learn really how to love. But romantic and sexual love can never be complete without *true* love.

While the only way to know what true love is, is to experience it, we can say that it has recognizable components: positive, accepting, and caring affection combined with appreciation and respect. Since words are so incapable of symbolizing it, you could probably add just as many descriptors yourself.

Perhaps a better way of explaining love is to point out what it is not. Misconceptions about the nature of love abound, and often it is a misconception which creates the problems, as it determines our actions and our expectations. We believe erroneously, so we behave incorrectly. Let me discuss some common misconceptions and try to clarify what true love really is.

"Love is feeling." This is such a commonly held misconception that I want to dispel it at the outset. "Feeling" here implies that love is some sentimental knot in the stomach which takes away your appetite and is only present if something special goes on inside you whenever you are near the love object. Or love is something you experience which is intensely strong and draws you to the other person with a force that is difficult to resist. You may still believe in love as feeling, but not define it quite as extremely—and you would still be wrong! Love has nothing to do with feelings. Feelings are the *consequence* of loving.

The damaging effects of such a notion are seen mostly in the area of marriage. All couples, I suppose, get married because they "feel" something in their love for each other. After a while this feeling diminishes or may even go away, and the conclusion one or both partners come to is that they are no longer in love. This expectation for some feeling to be perpetuated has led our society to develop a unique style of marriage in which there is a strong demand for a relationship of togetherness. It requires that there be a high degree of sharing and intimate relating. The success-fulness of this relationship thus determines the stability and longevity of the marriage. Lack of success usually results in the children paying the penalty, by the loss of a stable home.

The setting of so much value on shared intimacy—the demand for closeness—places a strain on marriage not conceived of in earlier times and certainly not seen in all cultures. Unfortu-nately, shared intimacy becomes equated with that special romantic feeling. When the feeling goes away, the conclusion is that there is nothing left on which to base love, and therefore the marriage must be dissolved. Because of an erroneous idea about the nature of love, true love and real intimacy have not de-veloped.

This is a *low view* of marriage. It is no wonder that such mar-riages can't hold together. Although it is quite true that in the

Figure 6

The Dimensions of Love

early stages of a romantically based love relationship, the feelings or emotions we experience predominate over everything else. This is only a part of the total love picture. True love has at least two other components to it: respect and acceptance, and a set of behaviors toward the love object. These dimensions are represented in Figure 6.

Without the *behaviors* toward the love object, love *feelings* would be meaningless. In fact, they could be so selfish that I doubt whether they would represent love at all. Lust would be in this category.

If you will examine 1 Corinthians 13 carefully, you will notice that everything described as "love" (which is the meaning of the word *charity* in some Bible versions) is related *not* to feelings, but to the other two dimensions of love, namely the behaviors toward the love object and the giving of respect and acceptance. It is possible, therefore, for the feeling component to be almost absent and yet for there to be a tremendously deep love present.

It also works the other way around. When a husband says to me, "I don't feel that I'm in love with my wife anymore," I usually reply, "When last did you behave toward her *as if you loved her?*" And then I see something remarkable happen. As soon as partners start behaving toward each other as if they still were in love, they begin to report that the feeling of being in love comes back. When they start being kind, patient, tolerant, unprovoking, and believing in truth, they feel in love again.

This has led me to ask whether the feeling dimension of love is the *consequence* of love behaviors rather than their cause. In other words, which comes first, the feelings or the behaviors?

You can prove this point quite easily (only in your imagination, I hope). Find someone you really love and start treating him or her as if you don't. Very soon (it's almost frightening how quickly) you begin to lose respect for the other party, and the feeling of love goes away. The reverse of this is also true. Would you like to try it and see?

Loving and liking. The second major confusion about love is in the area of "loving" versus "liking." Our lives are full of people we don't like. We don't like their habits, their mannerisms, their looks, the way they walk, talk, and even smell. Mostly we don't like them because we suspect that they don't like us, but for the moment let us assume that there are those we genuinely don't like. You ask:

"Must I love them?" *Yes!*

"Is it possible to love someone you don't like?" *Absolutely yes!*

"Can't I just ignore those people I don't like?" *No.*

"But I don't see how I can love someone I don't like." *Then hear me out.*

We are called to *love,* not to *like.* In fact, we are commanded to love the very objects we don't like. "Love your enemies," we are told. Can we like those who have our hurt and discomfort as their prime objective? That's what we are called to do.

I prefer to see liking as a bonus. If I like what I love, I am very fortunate. It's the icing on the cake. This is all the more reason why we must not get hung up on the feeling component of the dimensions of love. Love is what I must *do* to and for you. The feeling will take care of itself. If I love you, my enemy, I will soon begin to feel compassion, kindness, and respect for you. I can't help it; it's as if there were a law built into me that commands it.

Loving and hating.   "If I hate someone, I couldn't possibly be able to love him." This is the third misconception about the nature of love. Believing that love and hate are opposites—so that if you have the one, you can't have the other—has probably led to more breakups of relationships, especially marriages, than I care to count.

It is absolutely erroneous to believe that because you hate someone you can't love him. The truth of the matter is that what you hate you have a great capacity to love, and what you love you have a great capacity to hate.

Do you remember the song "You Always Hurt the One You Love"? Well, this is very close to the truth. The fact is, when you truly love somebody, you invest a lot of your being in that person and become extremely vulnerable because of the trust and commitment you make. If that trust is violated, you are likely to experience considerable emotional pain, and this can give rise to intense hate feelings. That's why, the more you love, the greater is your potential for hate. This is represented in Figure 7.

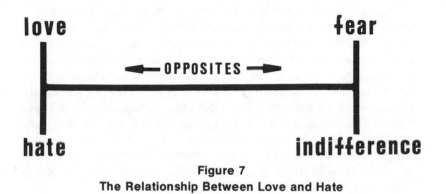

Figure 7
The Relationship Between Love and Hate

You will see that *love* and *hate* are together at one end of the pole. At the opposite end are *fear* and *indifference*. These two go together just as the other two do.

It is very important that we see fear, not hate, as the true opposite of love. "There is no fear in love; but perfect love casteth out fear . . ." John tells us in 1 John 4:18 KJV, thus setting fear as the opposite of love. Paul writes to Timothy: "For God hath not given us the spirit of fear; but of power, and of love, and of a sound mind" (2 Timothy 1:7 KJV).

When you fear someone, you can't love him—this is clear, because love and fear can't coexist. But notice that it is love that casts out fear. Again, it seems to me, we get the message that if we act out our love, the feeling (of fear, in this case) takes care of itself.

Just as fear is the opposite of love, indifference is the opposite of hate. At least when you hate someone, you care enough about him or her to have created an intense feeling of dislike, disgust, or dissatisfaction. But when you're indifferent, when the other person doesn't mean enough to you even to create any feeling of ill-will, love cannot be present.

How do we create love for those we hate? Jesus tells us in the Sermon on the Mount, "Love your enemies . . . *do good* to them that hate you" (*see* Matthew 5:44 KJV). In other words, behave as if you love, and the feeling of hate will take care of itself.

What I have been saying thus far has important implications for marriage relationships. Too often and too easily, couples conclude that their marriage is over, merely because they perceive that there is much hate feeling between them and therefore their love must be over. Look for the hate in your marriage and savor it, because it spells hope. When there is hate, there is great capacity for love. To transform hate into love, merely behave as if you do love and see this work miracles for the feelings. If your hate perpetually gets in the way, it means that you don't know how to love. Perhaps some professional counseling from a pastor or psychologist will help you understand where you are going wrong.

If you are caught at the opposite end of the pole in a fear-and-indifference trap, your situation is less hopeful—but not devoid of hope. Love *can* cast out fear and indifference. You *can* re-create the warm, accepting, and positive feelings that you so much desire. All you have to do is put action to your love wheels. Start behaving as if you love.

The Early Roots of Love Problems

Why do some find themselves with various love problems in adult life? Why do so many find it difficult either to give love or to receive it? The answer lies clearly in the early experiences of the person.

To make up for these deficiencies, such persons may resort to a number of strategies for defenses—and their personalities, to a large extent, are shaped by and reflect these strategies. Capturing love becomes a major life project for them, and everything they do and say becomes focused on this.

Our experience of love from the earliest years of life plays a major role in shaping who we become. If we are totally deprived of love for a prolonged period during our first year of life, we can become severely stunted psychologically. Physically, such a baby can lose weight and become lethargic, as if some defense system has alerted the organism to the fact that it has been delivered into a hostile environment. Nature would apparently rather remove the baby than leave him where he cannot be loved and nurtured.

As the child becomes more consciously aware of love in his early childhood, the potential for psychological damage increases. The child wants and needs love. If he is invited to receive love (which is what most parents do by manner and attitude) and is given unconditional love, he will develop a mature understanding of how love is given and received, and a stable and secure feeling is thus created. This can happen even when the environment is unsatisfactory, as in ghetto areas or in times or war when there is considerable threat to life. Somehow love protects the personality and breeds security under all conditions, no matter how adverse.

If, however, the child is invited to receive love and is hurt and punished as he approaches, severe conflict ensues. Sometimes this conflict is created merely by the inconsistency or unpredictability of the love. Double messages like "I love you—but I also hate you!" can be very provoking of deep-seated insecurity.

When these conflicts are severe, a child is placed in a double-bind situation where he is invited to receive love but cannot obtain it. This can produce the severest of all mental disorders and, according to some theorists, is the major cause of schizophrenia. Certainly, there are produced many dissociative states whereby the person begins to believe and also behaves as if he had more than one personality.

I certainly don't want any reader to engage in self-diagnosis and become alarmed. The disorders described are very severe and are seldom seen in everyday life. The most likely possibility is that you have experienced, like myself, much lesser extremes of love conflict and deprivation. Since children are remarkably resilient, the effects of this are seldom very severe—and usually only minor psychological scars are the consequence of this deprivation. If you believe that you may be suffering from one of the more severe emotional disorders, I strongly recommend that you seek professional help.

Of the less serious but still disturbing ways in which we try to cope with love deprivation in our early life, the following are most commonly seen:

1. A tendency to seek for love by . . .

- Excessively trying to please others.
- Continually putting oneself down and elevating others unrealistically.
- Becoming a "clinging person"—where the message is continually "Please love me," or "Please value me."
- Developing love substitutes such as extramarital affairs or falling in love repeatedly and very easily.

2. The development of severe character traits which become stamped deeply into one's personality . . .

- Excessive jealousy, where there is both an intense desire to be loved and a fear that the love will be withheld or lost.
- A tendency towards self-pity and remarkable skill at keeping oneself miserable so as to engage in self-punishment for the lost love.
- Sexual immorality, where there is a desperate search for love through sex.
- Pervasive insecurity, where extreme reactions are created by little things such as a spouse coming home late.

3. The development of a pain or illness to handle love deprivation . . .

"Now you'll have to love me 'cause I'm sick [or I'm in pain]" is the attitude. Love is captured primarily through sympathy. The "illness" can, of course, be purely psychological—though it may ultimately cause legitimate disease through the psychosomatic mechanism.

These are some of the pathetic ways in which people try to deal with their love deprivations. If a child is deeply and unconditionally loved and not given double messages or placed in a conflict situation over love, he can be spared these problems in later life. Love is a remarkably stabilizing keel. Hidden beneath the water, its weight and shape is such that, no matter how the strong winds of trouble may blow, it will always right the ship and keep it on its way.

When a child is deeply loved at home he can cope with teasing, being rejected by others, failure to meet performance demands, being poor, or lacking physical attractiveness. The sense of emotional security that love provides is deep and sure.

If a child is not loved at home, no amount of successes at sports, school prizes, and acceptance by peers can compensate. This child will grow up love-starved and love-distorted and will spend the rest of his life pathetically searching for love. If this should happen to you, I know of only one encounter that can adequately remove this distortion—it takes place beneath the Cross.

The Gospel and Love

The relevance of the Gospel to the problem of love has been noted by many writers. One of the unique features of Christianity is that it makes loving possible in the very face or rejection and persecution. In fact, central to the whole Christian understanding of love is the idea that love is only meaningful in the face of opposition and dislike. Jesus said, "For if ye love them which love you, what thank have ye? for sinners also love those that love them" (Luke 6:32 KJV). The call here is clearly to a much higher form of love, a love that transcends barriers of hate, dislike, fear, and indifference. This is a love that has no desire for personal reward—knowing full well that all the reward that love has to offer is in its giving and not its receiving.

When I am confronted by clients who are non-Christian, I am frankly pessimistic about how they will deal with their love problems. What models can they use? Where will they get their definitions of love? What resources do they have to draw on? Sometimes this very dilemma has caused them to ask me, "Well, where do you get your love from?" and I have had the privilege of sharing my experience with them. Being a Christian can make a big difference in what you believe love is all about.

How does the Gospel relate to the problem of love? I believe that the essence of its relevance is that is makes loving possible because of three new relationships—to *God,* to *others,* and to *ourselves.*

1. Loving is possible because of a new relationship to God.
Paul tells us that we are ". . . no more a servant, but a son; and
if a son, then an heir of God through Christ" (Galatians 4:7 KJV).
In the very next chapter he then lists *love* as the first of the fruits
of the Spirit.

God has demonstrated to the world that love can be unconditional and given to those who are undeserving of it, and we are
heirs of that giving. There is only one way you can know what
this is like—and that is to experience it for yourself.

**2. Loving is possible because of a new relationship to
others.**   Most of us have a hard time defining who our neighbor
is when we hear Jesus say that we must love our neighbor (*see*
Matthew 5:43). The Jews also had trouble, and that's why Jesus
told the parable of the Good Samaritan (*see* Luke 10:30–37).

Here *everyone* becomes our neighbor, without exception, even
those who have been our traditional enemies. Other people can
never seem the same, once we have encountered God in Christ.
Not only will we see them with different eyes, but we can love
them for a different reason. No longer do we have to depreciate
them in order to feel that we are worth something, nor do we have
to behave as if we love them just so that they will love us back.
Our love becomes unconditional because of the new relationship
we have with others through Christ.

Have you ever wondered why it is possible to love animals so
much more easily than human beings? Literally millions of
people shower love and affection on a wide range of pets from dogs
to little mice. I have always felt that there was something tragic
about this. Not that we should stop loving animals. I just adore
them, and there can be a lot of therapeutic value in having pets. A
number of psychiatric facilities are even providing pets for
psychotics and those with serious emotional disorders. Having
something to love and love you back can heal broken minds—and
we are discovering this truth at last!

But why is it so much easier to love pets? I think it's because
animals know only one way to love, and that is the *unconditional*
way. And we can love them because they will always receive that
love whenever it is given, without playing games or setting up
subtle resistances. Even when we have scolded them or withheld

their food, they will respond to the slightest show of affection with immediate pleasure and give no hint of any desire to get revenge or hurt us back. Why, even a completely strange dog can come up to me and begin receiving my love as if it were entitled to it. I would like people to do this also, but somehow they find it difficult.

3. Loving is possible because of a new relationship to ourselves. Encountering God changes our relationship to ourselves. No longer are we our own worst enemies. Our self-image ought to begin to undergo a drastic change. For the first time we can encounter a mirror that is thoroughly reliable and completely free of any distortion. We can see ourselves for what we are—valuable and precious. If we have been love-deprived, we can find the source of all love. If we have lived our lives in a constant state of self-hate, we can now surrender this hate. If we have pathetically sought the approval of others so as to feel that we are worth something, we can stop this search. If a parent has dominated our lives and caused us to feel that everything we do is just to please him or her, we can "replace" this parent with the Father who is all-loving and full of grace.

No longer can we relate to ourselves as we did before. No longer need we be self-destructive. We have been saved from ourselves—we are *free to love.*

Summary

We find it hard to give and receive love. The main reason is that we don't know what love is—and therefore we don't know how to love. Love is not just a feeling. A large part of love has to do with the behaviors we practice towards one another. A careful study of 1 Corinthians 13, the classic description of love, will reveal that it deals primarily with the behaviors of love. Love is action. Love is what we *do* to and for one another. The feeling dimension of love follows when we do loving things. Liking and loving must not be confused. We can love those we don't like, and in the act of loving we can come to like the object of our love.

Love and hate are not opposites but both aspects of love. The opposite of love and hate is fear and indifference. Where there is hate, there is a great capacity for love. Where there is love, there is a great capacity to hate.

We cannot love in the truest sense of the word until we have a new relationship to the Source of all love, to others, and to ourselves.

In closing, let me leave three further thoughts with you:

1. *Love is contagious.* Love begets love. If you feel that someone fears or hates you, then *you* should start the loving.

2. *Love and forgiveness go hand and hand.* If your desire to hurt back is strong, before you can begin to love you must first forgive.

3. *Loving others changes you.* You cannot remain the same as you were when you began to love—it's impossible. All you ever want to be can be realized if you start loving.

Additional Reading

1. *Start Loving.* Colleen Townsend Evans. New York: Doubleday.
2. *The Art of Loving.* Erich Fromm. New York: Harper & Row.
3. *Communicating Love Through Prayer.* Rosalind Rinker. Grand Rapids, Michigan: Zondervan.
4. *In His Steps.* Charles Sheldon. Old Tappan, New Jersey: Fleming H. Revell.
5. *Time for Love.* Eugene C. Kennedy. New York: Doubleday.
6. *Make Love Your Aim.* Eugenia Price. Grand Rapids, Michigan: Zondervan.
7. *The Greatest Thing in the World.* Henry Drummond. Old Tappan, New Jersey: Fleming H. Revell.
8. 1 Corinthians 13.

10

Freedom to Be Real

"What is REAL?" asked the Rabbit one day, when they were lying side by side near the nursery fender, before Nana came to tidy the room. "Does it mean having things that buzz inside you and a stick-out handle?"

"Real isn't how you are made," said the Skin Horse. "It's a thing that happens to you. When a child loves you for a long, long time, not just to play with, but REALLY loves you, then you become Real."

You may recognize this quotation from Margery Williams's *The Velveteen Rabbit,* the fascinating and moving story of a velveteen toy rabbit who so much wanted to be real but didn't know what "real" was. The story moves us because it causes us to identify with the dilemma of the toy rabbit. It triggers in us a question similar to the one he asks: "What is REAL?" It forces us to ask, "Am *I* real?"

It is not only toys that want to be real; people want to be real as well! Doesn't this seem strange to you? Compared to toys, we *are* real—or are we? I know this raises some philosophical questions, but the sense in which I want to use the word here relates to the longing we all have to become full, complete persons—people who know who they are and where they are going.

There is a quality of one's being that seems to be *unreal,* almost make-believe. We ask continually, "Is this really me? Is this all there is to me? Where do I fit into life? Am I in any way special?" We have a strong sense that we exist in order to become something, but we don't really know what that something is. Yes, the toy rabbit's dilemma strikes a chord of resonance in all of us, as it is an analogy to the deepest longings of all human beings.

Who Are You, Really?

One very prominent psychologist, Dr. Carl R. Rogers, has spent a lifetime trying to understand this dilemma. While I don't agree with everything that Carl Rogers has come to believe in his approach to understanding human nature, he has a very important point of emphasis that we should note. After thirty-three years in the psychotherapist's chair, encountering thousands of clients with their problems, he wrote this in *On Becoming a Person:*

> As I follow the experience of many clients, in the therapeutic relationship which we create, it seems to me that each one is raising the same questions. Below the level of the problem situation about which the individual is complaining, behind the trouble with studies, with wife, or employer, or bizarre behavior, or frightening feelings, lies *one* central search. It seems to me that at the bottom each person is asking: Who am I, really?

While I don't believe that Dr. Rogers has all the right answers, I do believe that he is right when he gives pride of place to the question *Who am I, really?* And the whole process of becoming real, of finding one's real self, is what most of life is all about. In some respects, this is what I have been trying to help you accomplish through this book. The process of becoming real is, I believe, what our Christian faith and walk are all about. It is a process (a sanctification, if you prefer) of finding yourself and, in a special sense, becoming real. I can find no better words to describe it.

Our Unreal Selves

"I suppose *you* are Real?" said the Rabbit. And then he wished he had not said it, for he thought the Skin Horse might be sensitive. But the Skin Horse only smiled.

Most of the time we deal with the outside world from behind phony façades. No one must know we aren't real, nor who we really are.

Why? Because we fear we won't be liked or accepted. There is something about our culture that prevents us from being real to the world. And the closer we are forced to live together, the more unreal we become and the more we hide from one another.

The way our society is now structured, with the majority of us living in urban areas where there has been an increased use of apartments and condominiums, we have been thrown together with a population density unknown in previous times. This has not improved our intimacy skills. If anything, we have become more skillful in finding psychological ways to distance ourselves and establish our privacy. It doesn't take bricks and mortar to build the most effective barriers between people, only psychological attitudes.

This diminished intimacy, despite our being forced to live closer together, has produced a quality of unreality in our relationships which was also probably unknown in previous times. It seems to me that when I was a child we knew more about the other people on our block than my children claim we now know. While this may be merely a cultural difference, since I have been in the United States I have checked this out with a number of people and all agree with me that this is their experience also.

Why are we so scared of being real to one another? I have already suggested that it is because we are afraid that others won't like what they see in the real us. But it goes a step further than this. Is it not possible that it is because we can't be real to ourselves? Because we are afraid of what we might see, we will not look deep within our own beings at what we really are. What is hidden in the deep recesses of our personality? What have we avoided accepting about ourselves? Why do we find it so uncomfortable when someone begins to be very honest with us about who we are? Because we are afraid of our real selves. We deny, we conceal, we ignore, and we resist every real truth about ourselves, especially if it is not attractive or desirable. If we can't be real to ourselves, how can we allow ourselves to be real to others?

> For a long time he lived in the toy cupboard or on the nursery floor, and no one thought very much about him. He was naturally quite shy, and being only made of velveteen, some of the more expensive toys quite snubbed him . . . . Between them all the poor little Rabbit was made to feel himself very insignificant and commonplace . . . .

Do you know this feeling?

We hide from our feelings. The struggle to become real is most evident with the emotions, because it is here that we want to hide from ourselves and from others. We are trained from our earliest years not to show our emotions—in fact, to be unreal.

Only a few hours ago I sat with a client who described how she had been taught not to display her anger. For many years she has been getting into trouble with other members of her family, her friends, and the people she works with because she cannot express her anger directly. She can only allow it to be expressed in passive, indirect ways like excessive pouting or criticism. The story she tells is: "I was told when I was a little girl that I should not show anger. 'People won't like you if you do' was the message I kept getting. So I spend my days sulking instead."

Because we are taught not to show feelings, some of us declare war on them and begin a campaign of suppression and denial that turns us more and more into toy people with no authenticity and no heart. We dare not allow ourselves to feel, so instead of being spontaneous and allowing joy and adventure to characterize us, we become stunted and overcontrolled. Because we must always hide our true feelings, we become an enigma. Instead of developing transparency so that all may know who and what we are, we become a mystery. Instead of finding wholeness and emotional health, we become erratic and unpredictable. No one can make sense of us, and everything we touch turns to unrealness. After all, when one person plays at being a toy, how do you expect anyone else to be real?

We depend on one another for reality. Whatever else it takes to set our *real* selves free, it can only happen in the context of our relating to one another. There is no way we can become real in isolation. We need people to make it happen. It seems to me that this is how God has ordained it, whether we like it or not. Why else would He have had so much to say about love? And forgiveness? And caring? It is only in our blending with one another that these can happen.

One of the most important lessons we are learning from the healing disciplines is that people who live in a real community become real themselves. Place psychotics in an accepting and understanding community, and they get better. Surround an alcoholic with support and caring, and he gives up his alcohol. Communities, we are discovering, can be powerful and therapeutic change agents.

Our society at large does not provide much in the way of community. Look at the titles of the books our age is producing: *The Lonely Crowd, The Pursuit of Loneliness, Pathways to Madness.* All of them deal with the loneliness of our time. We must surely be the loneliest society in all of history, and much of this loneliness is due to psychological barriers.

Why should this loneliness and psychological isolation prevent us from becoming real? Primarily because it prevents us from meeting our basic needs in a safe and stress-free manner. We all need to be loved, feel secure, be recognized, and have companionship—and these needs can only be met satisfactorily when we have significant "others" to whom to relate.

Our society is full of people who feel they are outcasts. Nobody really cares for them. If somebody does, it is usually because of a commitment through either marriage or family relationship: "You've got to love me; you have no alternative." Nobody cares for them unconditionally and without some obligation. Listen carefully to your neighbor or the person who sits next to you at work. The message you may get is one of loneliness and alienation and a desperate hunger for understanding at a deep level.

Carl Rogers identified three conditions that had to be present for people to become real or fully authentic. These conditions should be there as we grow up. If they are not, whenever we experience these conditions at some time later in life, we find something miraculous happening. In fact, Dr. Rogers went so far as to claim that a person cannot ever be fully himself unless these conditions are met:

- Unconditional acceptance and warmth
- Empathic understanding
- Congruence or genuineness

These qualities *heal* people—so much so that Rogers called them the "therapeutic triad." They provide a nonthreatening atmosphere in which people can explore and develop their true selves. Whenever relationships are characterized by these conditions, whenever communities foster these traits among their members, we turn from being artificial and phony into real people.

What actually happens when we begin to accept one another unconditionally with deep understanding and genuineness?

1. *We begin to experience, understand, and accept our feelings and desires that previously we would not consciously confront.* In our Christian communities, particularly, we tend to conceal our feelings of hostility and sexuality. Most of us live our lives feeling that we are hypocrites, because we fear that others are not quite like us and that the secrets of our feelings in these areas will somehow be discovered. It can be a revolutionary experience to discover, in the context of understanding and acceptance, that we are all in the same boat. Rather than being an excuse to indulge these further, this discovery frees us to achieve better control because of the accountability that the acceptance invites.

2. *We begin to understand the reasons behind our behavior and feelings.* The really free person is one who knows and understands *why* he does and feels things. Such people have been able to get behind the masks, façades and false fronts—that have been erected even to themselves—and thus know themselves better.

3. *We learn to be ourselves.* We discover that our real selves, despite their flaws and shortcomings, are all we have to offer to the world. So why not make the best of them? We learn not to fear ourselves and to confront our weaknesses and failures honestly and with enough courage not to punish ourselves. This opens us up to finding new and more positive forms of behavior, because

our energy is being directed at reconstruction and modification and not at self-destruction.

Who are you, really? You will only find out when you begin to encounter others with courage and openness. It's true that our society doesn't help us find our true selves, but why not begin by changing your tiny contribution to what society is. Start accepting others unconditionally, be understanding and genuine, and see if this doesn't pay off for you. You will be surprised how quickly others begin to do the same for you, and you will soon be on the way to becoming real. I'm trying it also!

> The Rabbit sighed. He thought it would be a long time before this magic called Real happened to him. He longed to become Real, to know what it felt like; and yet the idea of growing shabby and losing his eyes and whiskers was rather sad. He wished that he could become it without these uncomfortable things happening to him.

Are Our Christian Communities Any Better?

Theoretically, our Christian communities should be the ideal places for making people real. If you examine Dr. Rogers's therapeutic triad closely, you will see that the conditions he is advocating as necessary for healing are all captured by the New Testament concept of love. Love is all of these—unconditional acceptance, empathy and understanding, and genuineness. It is even more, but that will have to wait for another book.

What the Gospel gives us here, more than anything else, is a *reason* to be this way with one another. Perhaps this is what is wrong with our society—people don't have a reason to be any other way with one another. John reminds us that "We love him, because he first loved us" (1 John 4:19 KJV), and *because of this* we should love others. We cannot escape the principle that we must "Bear ye one another's burdens, and so fulfil the law of Christ" (Galatians 6:2 KJV). This is what gives us the incentive to care for one another. Why else would we do it?

But are our communities, our churches, our fellowships, our seminaries, and colleges loving and caring communities? You can

only answer this for yourself, because it would be unfair for me to
generalize. I do know, however that these communities are just as
full of lonely, alienated and outcast-feeling people as any secular
community I know.

We have been just as guilty of giving in to our natural inclina-
tions to hurt back and isolate others. We have emotional scars
from our past that get in the way of loving people; we have
learned how to shield and protect ourselves from the penetrating,
critical eyes of insecure people and developed our strategies for
forcing people away from us—and all of this despite our having
been loved first by the Source of all love.

Through my therapy office have passed as many hurting people
from Christian communities as from other communities. We have
no cause to be content with what is happening in our churches.
There is as much callousness, inconsideration, and selfishness in
the churches as anywhere else. It is often more easily concealed
behind masks and façades, that's all. And that is not the fault of
the Gospel. If the blame is to be put anywhere, it must be placed
squarely on ourselves. We distort our beliefs and excuse our mistakes, and most of what I have been saying in this book is directed
at correcting these distortions.

We have made our mistakes—so let's learn from them. We have
the incentive to love and care for one another—so let's remove
whatever hinders us. We have the power of God to transform
callousness, inconsideration, and selfishness into real acceptance,
understanding, and genuineness—so let's tap into the Source and
utilize it to make up for the deficiencies and inadequacies of our
own love ability. If you don't have any reason to want to love,
perhaps the problem is that you have never experienced His loving first. This, then, is where you should begin.

Weeks passed, and the little Rabbit grew very old and
shabby, but the Boy loved him just as much. He loved him so
hard that he loved all his whiskers off, and the pink lining to
his ears turned grey, and his brown spots faded. He even
began to lose his shape, and he scarcely looked like a rabbit
any more, except to the Boy. To him he was always beautiful,
and that was all that the little Rabbit cared about.

What Are the Characteristics of a Real Person?

The Rabbit could not claim to be a model of anything, for he didn't know that real rabbits existed; he thought they were all stuffed with sawdust like himself, and he understood that sawdust was quite out-of-date and should never be mentioned in modern circles.

As I have already mentioned, it is primarily in the area of the emotions that the struggle to become real predominates. What are the factors that influence this struggle and how can you move towards reality?

Authenticity. This implies that there is a consistency between what you are and what you pretend (or even believe) yourself to be. It is the result of knowing yourself realistically, not hiding any aspect of your being from yourself, and then being true to what you really are. Authenticity can only exist when you stop wanting to imitate someone else and when you are not overconcerned about the impression you make on others.

Phoniness is the opposite of authenticity and is characterized by a strong need to imitate the feelings, ideas, values, or attitudes of others. Sometimes these others are our parents, but often they are merely the significant group with which we relate, such as the people in our church or club.

Some people, in being phony, force themselves to be worse than they are. This can happen when someone wants to be "one of the boys" and engages in activities just to prove his masculinity. Others go the other way and become more hypocritical. Outwardly they display all the socially desirable signs which they feel their peer groups will admire, while deep within themselves their phoniness makes them sick.

To some extent, we all feel phony. That's part of our feeling of unreality. We feel so helpless when we try to be true to ourselves. Mostly we are afraid that people won't like what we really are, and therein lies our hang-up. I have struggled many times to convince various people that if they dropped their masks and revealed their true selves to the world, they would be much more accepted, *no matter what their true selves are like.*

Consider for a moment what it is you like about those people you really admire. Nine times out of ten, it is my guess that you admire their authenticity, their genuineness. What they are, and what they *say* they are, are highly congruent. "What you see is what you get!" Why, then, is it so difficult for *you* to be yourself? If you admire this trait in others, why should you be so afraid to risk being your authentic self?

I talked recently with a minister who described how he was struggling to measure up to the standards of the senior pastor of his staff. He agonized over his sermon preparation, trying always to make sure that he followed the rules for good sermons as he had learned them in seminary. But he was not succeeding. Somehow something was missing. He prayed earnestly, but he felt he could never match up, no matter how hard he tried. I asked him, "Have you ever tried just being yourself?" What did I mean? He was a man with so much to offer. His life had been full of experiences of both success and failure. My advice to him was: "Stop trying to imitate or compete with someone else, and let yourself come through what you have to say." Sermon techniques must be subservient to authenticity, and if he could achieve this, I felt strongly that he would feel better about his preaching. And he did!

Every one of us needs to be what he or she *uniquely* is. Being different from any other, we must discover how to be free to be ourselves. God did not cast us all in the identical mold, so why should we want to be like someone else? By this I don't mean that we should become bizarre or notorious. The antics of college students who seek to find their individuality through anti-establishment behavior is not what I am advocating. Frequently this behavior is motivated by a desperate search for identity and has nothing to do with one's uniqueness. We become what we are not, when we behave this way, not what we truly are. The young woman who becomes sexually promiscuous is not finding her true self, but running away from it.

The key to authenticity is to *be true to yourself.* Discover who and what you are through honest dialogue with trusting and accepting friends—and then be consistent with what you find.

Integrity. No one can be real if he does not do the right thing when no one else is there to judge. If he cannot keep the law when there is no policeman around, he does not have integrity.

For a person to have integrity, he must be responsible, reliable, and dependable to the values he lives by. These values are important because they determine our attitudes, thoughts, and behavior. Life has a way of forcing us to adopt values whether or not we are aware of them. Some values dominate us, while others operate with subtlety. While life is very complex and many situations arise where we do not have clear values to guide us, there are some basic values we should all have thought through carefully.

For instance, what is the value of material things to you? Are they a means to an end, or an end in themselves? Your answers here can determine how well you handle life's disasters. It is not my aim to force a particular value system on you. So whatever your system of values is, try to be true to it.

Adaptability. Life is like the wind. It can change direction without warning and is forever demanding that we adapt. To cope effectively with life we must be adaptable and resilient.

Adaptability implies that you can modify your style of life, expectations, and coping behavior to accomplish your goals, even when conditions are changing. Psychotics are not adaptable. They stick rigidly to their delusions and resist any hint that they should change. Neurotics are also less adaptable than normal people. They will persevere with nonproductive behavior patterns, often making the same mistake over and over again without learning from the experience.

To be adaptable, we must live in the present, facing realistically the facts of our lives. We must also believe that we have control over what we can do about a given situation and trust ourselves in the action we take. It may require compromise—not in the negative sense of giving up our basic values and surrendering freedom and individuality—but in the positive sense in which we realize that life is seldom a matter of blacks and whites, but rather grays. Not always can we say, "*This* is right, and *that* is wrong." More often, either way can be right, and we are left trying to delicately balance pros and cons in order to find the direction we should take. If we go one way, we give up some things. If we go another, we give up others. Compromise solutions cannot be avoided, and a willingness to be flexible is the only way to maintain one's sanity.

Resilience is what makes rubber different from other materials. Have you ever played with one of those "green monster" toys that you can stretch and twist beyond all recognition, and when you let it go it returns to its original shape? That's resilience. Without it life is miserable. To be resilient means you can bounce when life distorts you. When you receive a hard blow and your world seems to crumble, you can recover your composure and pick up from where you left off.

I once helped a man through the failure of his business. When he came to me he was ready to take his own life. Everything seemed hopeless. Not only had he lost all he owned, but so also did his parents and many of his friends. As a result of his failure, his immediate family no longer mattered to him. He couldn't face his children, let alone himself.

What can you say to someone in this situation? Very little. All you can do is trust that there is enough resilience for him to see some hope in his future and that he will bounce back.

And try again he did. Not too many months after this disaster, he began to rise to the challenge that the first failure had created. One failure doesn't make a catastrophe! What could he learn from this failure? Where did he make his mistakes? Hope began to rise again, and this time a wiser and much more adaptable man launched himself into business. In the process, he had come to terms with—and changed—his values. He had become a real person.

"Does it hurt?" asked the Rabbit.

"Sometimes," said the Skin Horse, for he was always truthful. "When you are Real you don't mind being hurt."

"Does it happen all at once, like being wound up," he asked, "or bit by bit?"

"It doesn't happen all at once," said the Skin Horse. "You become. It takes a long time."

Beginning to Be "Real"

Whatever way we look at it, being "real" is exactly what Christ wants us to be. Could I go so far as to suggest that ultimately your ability to be real depends on whether you allow Him to be in control of your life? How else can you be totally self-accepting? How else can you cut through your self-dishonesty and see your true self? How else can you determine your true value and bring yourself to the place of being willing and able to forgive yourself?

It is God, His Word, and His Spirit that create in us the desire to be honest with ourselves and show us where we can change and where we need to be self-accepting. It is God who gives us the ability and resources to change. He gives us a new perspective on ourselves as well as a new valuing of others, since we can now see them through His eyes. He gives us a reason to be forgiving. It is His humility, as demonstrated in Christ, that keeps our failures in perspective and prevents us from finding fault in others, merely to diminish the importance of our own inadequacies. God sets us on the way to becoming real by doing two important things for us:

He frees us. Romans 6:18 KJV says "Being then made *free* from sin, ye became the servants of righteousness" (italics added). This freedom to be real is crucial. What good is discovering your true self, as Dr. Carl Rogers advocates—including the experiencing of your feelings and the removal of your masks—if when you have found yourself, you still don't like what you see? You are then imprisoned by what you have found.

Even if you are no longer afraid of yourself, you are still not free. The beauty of the Gospel message is that when you have explored every ounce of your being, when all the dark corners have been illuminated and the total picture becomes clear, you are *set free* to become a new creation. You don't have to settle for the old. Trade it, if you will, for the new creation which God can offer you.

He transforms us. Romans 12:1, 2 makes this clear. The transformation takes place "by the renewing of your mind." Even as a psychologist I doubt if I could explain all that is implied in this "renewing" of the mind. I know that it can mean a major upheaval and that our values can change drastically. Suddenly we can tell the essentials of life from the nonessentials, so that we don't have to clutter up our emotions with reactions to that which is trivia in God's sight. We establish new priorities so that we change "I ought to" into "I want to," and each unnecessary "I've got to" in life becomes secondary to "What does *God* want me to?" We also have a clearer understanding of our obligations to others.

So, when you are freed and transformed you have laid the essential foundations for becoming real. You now have the potential for becoming all the things that Carl Rogers and others have so clearly identified as being the essence of reality:

- Genuinely authentic
- Openly transparent
- Acceptingly tolerant
- Comfortingly understanding
- Empathically responsive
- Honestly integrated
- Flexibly adaptable

If you examine these qualities closely, you will see that they are all aspects of the fruits of the Spirit. The tragedy seems to be that Dr. Rogers and other psychotherapists have clients more willing to develop these qualities than the Holy Spirit has obedient and pliable disciples.

"Give me my Bunny!" [the Boy] said. "You mustn't say that. He isn't a toy. He's REAL!"

When the little Rabbit heard that he was happy, for he knew that what the Skin Horse had said was true at last. The nursery magic had happened to him, and he was a toy no longer. He was Real. The Boy himself had said it.

That night he was almost too happy to sleep, and so much love stirred in his little sawdust heart that it almost burst.

Barriers to Becoming Real

With all the good intentions in the world, you could still end up spending your life in the toy cupboard. What are some of the

barriers that could prevent you from becoming real and what
can you do about them?

Beliefs and expectations. I am a great believer in the value
of stretching one's potential by attempting the little extra. It is a
good exercise for coming to know our limits. "Reach for a star and
perhaps you'll catch a cloud" is a good attitude—up to a point. The
problem is that some of us tend to want to reach for a star in
another galaxy. We are far too unrealistic in setting our goals and
ambitions, with the consequence that we set ourselves up for repeated failure. This can have devastating effects on our quest for
our true selves. If the ratio of our failures to our successes is too
high, we are liable to become despondent and discouraged, as well
as confused about who we really are.

The solution is to trim back your expectations to a more realistic level. If you are not an Einstein, be content with passing
Physics I. If you are not a Billy Graham, be content with preaching at your tiny church. You cannot become what you are not—
only what you are—and while many could become more than they
are by stretching their dreams a little, this should be tempered
with a recognition of one's limits.

Let me put it another way. If you know yourself honestly, you
can set realistic goals for yourself. If you don't, you are likely to
increase the ratio of your failures to your successes by attempting
too much and consequently will only become more frustrated and
confused. Make your aim, therefore, realistic self-knowledge and
complete self-acceptance.

An unsatisfactory environment. You are not always to blame
for what happens to you. Sometimes you can be the victim of
circumstances. You may have made the best decisions possible at
the time, about work, school, relationships, moving, but somehow
everything has gone sour. What frequently happens then is that a
"learned helplessness" (a phrase coined by Dr. Seligman) takes
over. Thereby you are immobilized, or so it seems, and cannot
take any steps to get out of the unsatisfactory situation. It's as if
you were paralyzed and could not move a mental muscle. You go
back again and again, as if something were forcing you to persevere. I've known women who continue to receive severe beatings
from their drunken husbands and feel completely helpless to

avoid the situation. And what about the emotional beatings many take in work situations? Under these conditions you cannot become real. You are like a tiny ship tossed about on a fierce sea over which you have no control.

The first step to reality is, obviously, to deal with your helplessness. It may mean having the courage to change your situation; it may mean becoming more assertive and claiming your legitimate rights (without denying anyone else his). To become real *you* must take full responsibility for your life and implement whatever steps are necessary to put this responsibility into action. I don't believe God encourages "learned helplessness." He intends that we should use the resources He has provided. So rise up, take control, and claim these resources. Just having the feeling that you are taking control of yourself is sufficient to dispel the helplessness.

> "It takes a long time [to become Real]. Generally, by the time you are Real, most of your hair has been loved off, and your eyes drop out and you get loose in the joints and very shabby. But these things don't matter at all, because once you are Real you can't be ugly, except to people who don't understand."

Summary

We all long to know who we are—to become full, complete persons who are *real* to ourselves and to others. We often hide from our true feelings and depend on our relationships with others for our sense of reality.

Authenticity of self-identity is best developed under conditions of acceptance, understanding, and genuineness. We can help to achieve this by encountering others with courage and openness.

A Christian who accepts the basic tenets of God's love and forgiveness can not only come to better terms with himself but can be better equipped to cope with the feeling of isolation which is so prevalent in today's society. Authenticity, integrity, and adaptability are developed as we let God release us from our emotional prisons. The Source frees and transforms us and provides the strength to overcome the barriers to becoming real, as we learn to set realistic goals and deal with unsatisfactory conditions in everyday life. Paradoxically, as we abandon ourselves to God, we are freed to realize our full potential.

Additional Reading

1. *The Velveteen Rabbit.* Margery Williams. New York: Doubleday.
2. *On Becoming a Person.* Carl R. Rogers. Boston: Houghton Mifflin.
3. *Why Am I Afraid to Tell You Who I Am?* John Powell. Niles, Illinois: Argus Communications.
4. *Life More Abundant.* Charles L. Allen. Old Tappan, New Jersey: Fleming H. Revell.
5. Ephesians 2.

Epilogue

I BEGAN THIS BOOK by emphasizing that feelings are a part of life. We cannot escape them, though many find ways to circumvent and distort their experience of them. My message has been a simple one—feelings are our friends and they should neither imprison us nor be imprisoned by us. Knowing how to experience them, own up to them, and even control them when necessary is essential to mental health—and emotional freedom.

I have taken you on a journey through some of your emotions and by now probably have readers with a number of different reactions. I hope that for most of you it has been an enlightening journey. You have discovered new aspects of your personality and identified the mistakes you most commonly make in the realm of your emotions. You have moved towards becoming more real, fully human yet fully spiritual, fully emotional yet fully victorious over your emotions. But some of you may be even more frustrated over your emotional problems. Whether you are being successful or whether you are still struggling with your emotional growth, I would like to make some closing remarks which may be helpful to you.

1.   Perhaps you are saying to yourself: *This is too painful. Becoming a real, emotionally free person seems to hurt more than staying as I am.*

This is true. It may well be more hurtful to change than to stay as you are. But the pain is short-lived, and the freedom which follows is well worth the effort. Psychological growing pains are inevitable. It would be nice if our emotional growth (and our spiritual growth also, for that matter) was continuous and steady from beginning to end. Unfortunately, it comes in irregular fits and starts—often, I suspect, because we resist change and per- petuate self-destructive behavior without realizing what we are doing. If you are suddenly confronted by a need for change, have the courage to make the change, even if you find it painful to do so. It can be helpful to remember the following:

DON'T EXPECT TOO MUCH OF YOURSELF TOO SOON. This is a com- mon mistake, even for those undergoing psychotherapy: to want to effect too much change too soon. There is no quick and easy road to emotional maturity. Be patient with yourself. You have not learned your present behavior patterns overnight, so don't expect them to vanish that quickly.

DON'T EXPECT COMPLETE SUCCESS. Some failures are inevitable, and these are just as necessary for psychological growth as are your successes. Failures are to grow by. Failures pinpoint the weak spots and show where the defenses need to be strengthened. On the other hand, don't be content with your failures, but use them as important learning experiences to make the necessary adjustments and corrections to your present behaviors.

DON'T BECOME DISCOURAGED. Keep experimenting with the ideas I have outlined and find new strategies more applicable to your life situation where necessary. You will often feel most dis- couragement just before the breakthrough to success—so re- member this before you allow your discouragement to cause you to give up.

2. Perhaps you are saying to yourself: *I think I'm better off staying as I am—in my emotional shell.*

A client recently began to risk changing her behavior and relat- ing to her friends in a more authentic, loving, emotionally real way. One little incident backfired and didn't work out just as she expected, so she panicked and pulled back into her emotional shell. "I'll just not trust anyone again. It's *safer* that way," she told me. It took me many sessions to get her back to the point of willingness to take a risk in giving love to others, and eventually she did succeed. But I won't be around to help you overcome your first obstacle. True, it may seem safer to stay as you are, but in the long run the risks you must take will pay their rewards. Trust God to give you the courage that you will need to try over and over again.

3.   Perhaps you are saying to yourself: *It's all very well for more capable and competent people—they can change and become emotionally real. I just don't have what it takes.*

It's possible, I suppose, for some to have read through this book and still have such a defeatist attitude. However, I would be more concerned if you felt completely capable and fully competent to do everything I have outlined by yourself. To feel a measure of inadequacy is more normal than to feel fully competent.

One of the central tenets of the Christian faith is the idea that as human beings we are basically inadequate. It is a delusion to think that we—in ourselves—are totally competent for emotional healthiness. It is unnecessary to pretend either to ourselves or to others that we are totally self-sufficient, for we are not. We need God in our lives, and real freedom only comes from total surrender to the living God as helpless, dependent persons. This is the paradox of our humanity—the more dependent we are on God, the more freedom we experience to be ourselves fully.

So in all you seek to do for yourself—for every exercise of loving, for every act of coping with your anger or depression, for every thought controlled and channeled towards constructive emotions—trust and depend on God. Abandon yourself to Him, and you will be freed to fulfill all the potential that is in you.

This is real freedom!

Index

Hippocrates 96

Honesty 18, 20, 21, 81, 88, 90, 113, 119, 121, 128, 130, 142, 167, 174, 177–179

Horney, Karen 136

Hostility 50, 61, 71–75, 78, 79, 84, 87, 88, 92–94, 170

Humanness 17, 18, 23, 24, 29, 32, 33, 39, 40, 42, 43, 50, 67, 68, 70, 79, 89, 118, 126, 141, 151, 162, 166, 183

Hume, David 136

Humiliation 68, 75, 86, 119, 127, 177

Hurt 15, 23, 64, 68, 69, 74–76, 80–82, 84–94, 120, 121, 139, 140, 142, 156, 159, 163, 164, 172, 176, 183

Ideas 17, 38, 48, 55, 56, 59, 64, 91, 92, 98, 109, 110, 113, 117, 124, 138, 145–147, 161, 173, 184, 185

Imprisoned 9

Inauthenticity 17

Inconsiderate 79

Insomnia 36

Insult 56

Intellectualizing 30

Intimacy 19

Irrational ideas 48, 140, 149

Irrational thoughts 20, 32, 42, 44, 57, 109, 130, 131, 141, 144, 145, 147

James, William 27, 28

Jealousy 31, 32, 51, 160

John 2:13–17 93

1 John 4:8 152

1 John 4:18 157

1 John 4:19 171

1 John 4:20 152

1 Kings 18 96

1 Kings 19:4 96

1 Kings 21 96

Learned helplessness 179

Leviticus 16:20–22 70

Life of faith 10

Life-style 35, 37, 61, 63, 64, 69, 73, 81, 95, 101

Love (see chapter 9), 160–165, 169, 171, 178, 184, 185

Loss 31, 36, 101–107, 109–114

Luke 6:32 161

Luke 10:30–37 162

Manipulation 68, 69, 139, 140, 144

Mark 3:5 93

Mark 12:30 118

Marriage 39, 62, 153, 154, 156, 158, 169

Masks 170, 177

Matthew 5 84

Matthew 5:38–48 82

Matthew 5:43 162

Matthew 18:21–35 90

Matthew 23:13–39 93

Maturity 62, 67, 88, 184

May, Rollo 136

Medication 39, 97, 98

Menninger, Karl 147

Mental health 29

Minds 29

Misconceptions 29, 40

Misery 24, 39, 44, 52, 61, 70, 71, 89, 97, 102, 110, 135, 151, 160, 176

Misunderstood 11

Motivating 86

Neurosis 19, 33, 42, 66, 101, 133, 135, 136, 143, 144, 145, 148, 175